Vintage and Iconic Aircraft

NEW ZEALAND COLLECTIONS

DON JESSEN

Bateman

Text © Don Jessen 2016

Published in 2016 by David Bateman Ltd
30 Tarndale Grove, Albany, Auckland, New Zealand

www.batemanpublishing.co.nz

ISBN 978-1-86953-947-4

Publisher: Bill Honeybone
Photographs by Marilyn Jessen, except those listed on page 327
Book design: Cheryl Smith, Macarn Design
Printed in China through Asia Pacific Offset Ltd

Vintage and  *Iconic Aircraft*

CONTENTS

FOREWORD

Another book about aeroplanes ... Yes, I know there have been plenty, but this one is from a guy well-versed in vintage-themed stories, having written three other books about caravans and lovely old boats. Don Jessen's father and uncle were in the RNZAF during World War II. His dad was an engineer, his uncle a Lancaster bomber pilot. Many of us who fly and love aeroplanes have similar stories, and this text will keep some of those stories alive in perpetuity. Herein lies a pictorial and anecdotal legacy of some of our wonderful aviation history. From the oft-controversial first-ever flight of Richard Pearse, to profiles of our air force, our museums, our internationally acclaimed airshows, to high-school students building aeroplanes — it all adds up to a fabulous exposé of New Zealanders' passion for flight.

The farm next door is fertilised by a Fletcher topdresser. In a hangar next to where I live is a homebuilt microlight, and a gyrocopter. Graham Orphan's engaging, illustrious *Classic Wings* is read across the Southern Hemisphere and beyond. And Sir Peter Jackson and Gene De Marco present the world with pristine, authentic and nimble little World War I fabric-clad fighters. New Zealand loves flying, and the world loves New Zealand.

My dad flew Spitfires in Burma, as a photo reconnaissance (PR) pilot. I still remember, as a barefooted kid, his service revolver sitting in a top drawer in his bedroom on our Taranaki dairy farm. He wore his leather sheepskin flying jacket 'feeding out' in winter, until it wore out. Like many of you, I followed my father and became a pilot. I bought a Yak-52, and was both flattered and thrilled to fly a warbird trainer. I learned formation and aerobatic flying from one of New Zealand's best: Brett Emeny. Rated in over 110 types of aircraft, including the P-51 Mustang, the Hunter jet and the P-40 Kittyhawk, Brett owns and flies his own Vampire, Trojan, Yak-52, Auster and glider, and several others. He has just restored, and flies, our sole Catalina flying boat. And he has happily taught countless pilots to fly.

My love of aeroplanes and coffee spawned the idea of an aviation café, themed with genuine aircraft parts, airmen's stories and uniforms, and great food and beverage. I'm thankful that we now co-own two — in Queenstown and New Plymouth airports.

I thank Don for the opportunity to share this passion. This is not the definitive text on New Zealand aviation history. It's a snapshot of how much we love to fly, of how much our country was made for flying, and is a wonderful 'pilot's pot-pourri' of pictures and rich little stories.

I hope you enjoy them all.

Jim Hickey
New Plymouth, 2016

INTRODUCTION

I have always been interested in aeroplanes, especially old aircraft, and even more specifically warbirds. When growing up, I, along with my father, had a substantial library of aircraft books. I then learned to fly in the mid-1970s, completing 49 hours' flying time towards a private pilot's licence before career and marriage and mortgages took over.

My father had volunteered as a pilot at the beginning of World War II, but when it was found out that he was a motor mechanic he was immediately moved into the role of an aircraft engineer. During World War II, he trained on the airframes and engines of Tiger Moths, Kittyhawk fighters and Hudson bombers. His younger brother, Bob, (previously a barber) had been a Lancaster pilot, so I grew up listening to fascinating stories about these iconic aircraft.

When I started this project I knew I wanted to cover from very early aircraft through to World War II and some of the iconic post-war aircraft. However, I did not realise how vast this topic was, and how many fantastic old aircraft we have here in New Zealand. My interest in, and knowledge of, vintage and reproduction aircraft, and the work involved

to restore or construct them, has increased 10,000-fold. I have come across aircraft that I did not know even existed, yet alone were flying or being restored or re-created in New Zealand. I have also come across aircraft that I definitely had preconceived notions about, on which I have been completely re-educated. Along the way I have come across some 'ghosts of the past' that have connections with our family.

I have been privileged to meet some very knowledgable people, some incredible characters and some brilliant pilots. They have given freely of their time and have told me some great stories, filling my head with details of these fantastic aircraft. I am truly indebted to these people who build stunning reproductions of vintage aircraft, and restore, collect and fly wonderful old planes. They are a breed apart, and without their input this book could not have been written. Along the way I have found out a huge amount about my uncle's flying career during the war, along with a heap about my own father's war service in the Royal New Zealand Air Force (RNZAF).

I have talked to pilots whose flying hours number in the many thousands of hours, and who have flown and continue to fly so many different types of aircraft that one's head reels with what they impart. With these pilots, flying is in their blood. Some of them fly for a living, then jump in vintage aircraft to fly for leisure and pure pleasure. Others have retired from commercial flying, but continue to clock up hours in these amazing old aeroplanes. Some pilots have come up through the private pilot licence (PPL) system and have graduated to flying these wonderful aircraft, some of them getting so keen that they have gone out and bought one, or become part of an ownership syndicate. Still others, who are not pilots, have become enamoured with these vintage aircraft and just love being around them, helping out at airshows, open days and with minor maintenance and club activities.

Thanks to Sir Peter Jackson's passion for World War I fighters, New Zealand probably has the world's best collection of aircraft from this particular era. Sir Peter makes this collection available to the public through the museum at Hood Aerodrome in Masterton. Through the summer there are opportunities to attend open days and view these aircraft flying. There is only a very small band of highly experienced pilots who are capable of flying them, and even they say that the experience is very different from what they have been used to. I was lucky enough to talk to a 'newbie', and his account of his first flight in one of these historic aircraft was one of pure excitement.

Many of the other associations that are flying aircraft from the 1930s to the 1960s also have open days, and they, too, are well worth attending. Even standing on terra firma watching these aircraft fly, and walking around them, can transport you back in time, and you just wonder at the technology of the period, the bravery of the pilots and what it must have been like to be a pilot or aircrew in those times.

With some of the aircraft featured, you can actually pay and go for the ride of your lifetime. How cool would that be!

Along with all of the 'civilian' aviators, I have been privileged to be able to bring our own RNZAF on board, featuring not only the Wigram-based museum and the newly restored static World War II Oxford, but also the famous Hercules and Orion aircraft that have been used, and still are used, by many air forces across the world. The Hercules recently celebrated 61 years of continuous manufacture. These iconic aircraft have gone through many technical upgrades throughout their lives, and have both become legends of the air. Their New Zealand stories alone are incredible.

One of the most challenging aspects of writing this book was not as I thought it would be — finding enough aircraft to put in the book — but rather deciding which aircraft of the many available to profile. I have deliberately chosen to provide a taste of the wide and diverse range of iconic, rare and vintage aircraft that we have in New Zealand, and a tiny taste of a few of the incredible pilots who fly these stunning aeroplanes. A snapshot of New Zealand vintage aviation, so to speak.

In listing the aircraft through the years, I have opted to use the date on which the model was first produced, as opposed to the date of the individual featured aircraft. Some aircraft had just a few short years of production, others a very long production period. For instance, some started production before World War II and finished several years post-war. We have one model that started in 1931 and finished in 1948. The

two aircraft featured look identical, but one was produced in 1934 and the other in 1947! So the easiest way was to start as I have, with the first production year of the model concerned.

It is my hope that this book will appeal to both the enthusiast and the general public. We have a fantastic aviation history in New Zealand, and an amazing restoration, reproduction and replica industry. Our reproduction and replica planes and restorations are world-class. I am both honoured and privileged to have been able to showcase some of these iconic aircraft in this book, and to tell the stories of some of our most colourful pilots who fly these wonderful machines. And, I must admit, I have had an absolute blast researching and writing this book. There are an enormous number of people I need to thank, for providing information, allowing me access to their beautiful aircraft, and sharing their stories. To all of the 'aviation guys and gals', a heartfelt thank-you for making the journey so much fun!

Don Jessen
Hamilton, 2016

IN THE BEGINNING... RICHARD PEARSE

In the beginning, when man dreamed of flight, there was the hot-air balloon. Then came the engine-powered dirigible, more commonly known by the name Zeplin. But man still dreamed of a powered craft with wings that could fly in the sky like a bird. On 17 December 1903, Wilbur and Orville Wright made history when they flew their warped-wing biplane in a controlled takeoff, controlled straight flight of 120 feet, followed by a controlled landing. They were credited with being the first men to successfully build and fly an aircraft, and their names were forever written in the history books. But were they the first?

On the other side of the world, deep down in the South Pacific in Aotearoa, in the land of the long white cloud, New Zealand, a young man had been looking skyward and dreaming of building a flying machine, as early as 1898. His name was Richard Pearse, a reluctant farmer who was happiest when he was in his shed making mechanical things. He designed a flying machine, figuring that he needed a very light but powerful engine to power the craft. As there was nothing available, he designed and built his own engine. By 1901, the engine was reputably built and he started on the aircraft, using light steel, wire and bamboo for the framing, with fabric covering the wings. Using a sling seat and a warped wing, he attempted his first flight on 31 March 1902. As soon as he lifted off, the aircraft lurched to the left and crashed. A re-think was needed. Subsequently, he designed and fitted the world's first ailerons (flaps), extending the wings to accept the flaps/airbrake, and attached a steerable tri-cart to the mono-wing. It was, in fact, a complicated ancestor of some of the early microlights, just built some 70 years previously.

His next witnessed flight apparently took place in March 1903, where he flew for 450 feet before crashing into a gorse hedge, some 15 feet off the ground. A repeat of this flight was made on 2 May 1903, with exactly the same result.

On 11 May, taking off on the road running alongside Opihi River, Richard became airborne, completed a left turn, flying over a 30-foot river bluff, before completing a right turn and flying parallel to the river. According to witnesses, he covered more than 3000 feet before his engine seized and he was forced to crash-land.

A replica of Richard Pearce's aircraft is housed in the Museum of Transport and Technology (MOTAT) in Auckland. Even better than that is a carefully researched reproduction of Pearse's aircraft that has been built over a number of years by retired automotive engineer Ivan Mudrovcich.

A few months later the Wrights made their historic flight and, with many others getting into the picture, Richard quietly put his plane to bed. He always said his flights were uncontrolled because of the crash-landings, and he never contested the official history of 'firsts'. Yet here was a young farmer-cum-inventor who designed both a plane and its engine with very few resources, and was most probably the first person in the world to fly an aeroplane. In 1909, Richard built a larger aircraft, so clearly he did not lose interest in aviation.

For many years Richard Pearse's efforts were lost in the mists of time, until one of our most famous pioneer pilots, George Bolt, decided to track down what had actually happened. The above story is pretty much an account of what he discovered. The story is based on eyewitness accounts, including those of Richard's younger brother, who swung the propeller. All of those people are now long gone. So did Richard actually fly? Did he get off the ground? Or was his aircraft incapable of flying? There seems to still be some controversy about what actually happened: some people discredit the story, while others passionately believe that he did accomplish man's first powered flight. Whatever your belief, it is fact that the aeroplane did actually exist. This early aeroplane epitomises the ingenuity and number-8-wire intellect that New Zealanders are renowned for, and which places this fair country of ours right at the forefront of man's dream to fly like a bird. Something we should all be immensely proud of. Maybe the highly detailed and researched reproduction of Richard Pearse's aircraft and

engine, painstakingly built over many years by Ivan Mudrovcich, will finally give us the answer.

As a footnote, another American, formerly a German immigrant, Gustave (Weisskopf) Whitehead, is reputed to have made a powered flight in Connecticut on 14 August 1901, with several more flights before the Wright brothers. Like Richard Pearse, his flights are surrounded in controversy. There were supposed witnesses and the flight was written up at the time in a local newspaper. The Wright brothers, along with others in authority, say Whitehead's aircraft never flew. Again, however, there is no question that his aircraft actually existed.

It seems to me that we have, in fact, three contenders for the crown of man's first powered flight, and no real way of concluding who was first. There is certainly enough evidence to bring into question the Wright brothers' claim, but not enough evidence to conclusively prove who may have been first. Both Whitehead and Pearse are now recognised as having played an important part in aviation's development, therefore substantiating the fact that they both had built aircraft. But no one has gone as far as changing the accepted history. Still, there is nothing like a good mystery to get us all thinking!

The Pearse Reproduction Aircraft

Ivan and Janel Mudrovcich have been on a 12-year journey, during which time they have almost finished building an authentic reproduction of Richard Pearse's first aircraft. Through the writing of this book, I have engaged in conversation and interviewed some incredible people and seen some equally incredible aircraft, but this one was something very special.

Ivan originally decided to build a reproduction engine. After much research and time spent measuring the original parts of the Richard Pearse engine that had been dug out of the ground by George Bolt, Ivan was able to draw an authentic plan. It is a horizontally opposed, double-action two-cylinder engine. It is a low-powered, low-revving engine, but is a genuine reproduction. As a tradesman, I can truly appreciate the quality of Ivan's workmanship. I am astounded at

the ingenuity and skill of Richard Pearse in creating this engine. He was forging new ground with it. The current reproduction engine is a testament to both Richard and Ivan, although Ivan modestly says that all he did was research the engine, then copy what Richard Pearse had built. That may be so, but the understanding of Pearse's thinking and the skill to reproduce the engine are not to be taken lightly.

With the engine built, Ivan sought out someone to build an authentic reproduction aircraft. He was keen to fit the engine and see if the thing would actually fly. After talking to a few people, looking at replica models, and carrying out his own research, Ivan said to Janet, 'I think I might have to build the aircraft myself.'

During his research, Ivan had found a reporter's interview script with Pearse. When the reporter had asked about camber in the wings, Pearse had replied that the wings did not have a camber, they were arched. The reporter subsequently wrote in his piece that the wings had no camber, which many later researchers took to mean that the wings were flat. More indepth research undertaken by Ivan revealed that this conclusion was incorrect, and that the wings had a substantial curvature or 'arch' to them. So began the actual aircraft build. I have seen the completed aircraft with the engine fitted, and it is a stunning piece of work. With its 40-foot wingspan, it looks very impressive. From its massive wing to the fine work in the tricycle undercart, every detail has been meticulously researched and built to be as authentic as it can possibly be.

On Ivan's first taxi run, he started the engine and, with propeller spinning, the aircraft just sat there, not moving at all. He called to his son to give him a push. A 20-foot push was all that was needed to get the Pearse reproduction taxiing under its own propulsion. Ivan soon realised that the primitive engine needed a combination of airflow and headwind, and that the exhaust valve needed to open and shut at the correct time and speed in order to even think about getting lift-off.

Ivan describes the engine: 'By today's standards it's a most horrible engine — a bucket of bolts.' That's his way of saying that it is primitive, has a low power band, and is complicated to get everything in sync. 'However,' Ivan adds, 'over 100 years ago it would have been very advanced.'

Part of the wing has been air-tunnel-tested, and those reports, along with the independent verbal reports I have had of the latest taxiing effort at Whitianga, have suggested that this aircraft is capable of flying. Indeed, if it was fitted with a lightweight low-powered aircraft engine of modern design, it most likely would have flown by now. But, as Ivan says, 'That's not the point. The actual point is to build an authentic reproduction of both engine and aircraft, to see if indeed we can get it to fly. I think I know what has to be done to the engine to create a little more consistent power, then it's matching the wind conditions needed to achieve some kind of flight.'

I have absolutely no doubt that Ivan and his team will achieve their goal in the not-too-distant future.

THE PIONEER YEARS AND THE GREAT WAR

The 10 intervening years between man's first recorded flight and World War I saw the development of aircraft progress slowly. Over 50 different aircraft were designed and flown, with varying degrees of success. By 1910, aeroplanes, although rare, were becoming accepted. Man had conquered the air and could fly like a bird. By today's standards, though, these aircraft were crude and fragile.

Back in New Zealand, a South Islander by the name of Bert Pither, who was known for his love of manufacturing anything weird and mechanical, built a Bléroit-style aeroplane of his own design. It is reputed to have flown in 1910. Two brothers, Vivian and Leo Walsh, built a British Howard Wright biplane, which Vivian went on to fly on 5 February 1911. Vivian was an engineer by profession, but, after this first officially-recognised powered flight in New Zealand, the brothers went on to form The New Zealand Flying School. By 1915, they were building their own series of flying-boat trainers, and were deeply involved in training New Zealand pilots for the Royal Flying Corps.

The outbreak of World War I accelerated the development of the aeroplane, and by the end of the war famous names of aircraft had emerged as great fighter planes, along with many national heroes on all sides. These early fighter pilots were considered Knights of the Sky, with many becoming legends, along with the planes they flew. Unfortunately, life expectancy was measured in days or weeks for many, and in months for the extraordinary pilots. Those pilots who survived the Great War did so against great odds.

We are fortunate in New Zealand to have a small band of enthusiastic people who have gone out and created the amazing Aviation Heritage Trust Museum in Masterton and the Omaka Aviation Heritage Centre in Blenheim. Both feature many static and many flying restored and reproduction World War I planes. The museums, along with The Vintage Aviator Ltd, who actually restore old aircraft and build exact flying reproductions of World War I aircraft, are responsible for the fantastic collections of World War I planes that we have in New Zealand. They are absolutely world-class. The people involved are super-talented engineers, enthusiasts, owners and pilots. To see these aircraft on display, on the ground and flying is awe-inspiring, and gives us a taste of what it must have been like in those early days. Likewise, the Omaka Aviation Heritage Centre is remarkable in that it tells the story of the aerial development and the war in the most graphic way imaginable.

This leads us into featuring some of these remarkable aircraft that can be seen flying in New Zealand skies.

PITHER MONOPLANE
1910 (REPLICA)

As I was exploring the Croydon Aviation Heritage Centre at Mandeville, I came across what appeared to be a very early aircraft. I walked around her in astonishment. She looked to be an earlier model than some of the very early Great War aircraft that I had previously seen. After enquiring about her, I found that the Croydon Aircraft Company staff, under the able leadership of Colin Smith, had built a replica of H.J. (Bert) Pither's 1910 bicycle-steel-framed monoplane in order to put his designs to a practical test. The replica is powered by an aero engine built by Bill Sutherland, of Waikaka. The design is a replication of the original unusual V4 engine, and can be set to model the original output as described by Pither.

The aim of the project was to honour this very inventive man for his engineering achievements, and, in particular, to do so as he was a Southern man. The detailed plans for the replica were drawn up from photographs and newspaper reports. She has an exposed steel-frame fuselage with steel tubing and wooden ribs in the wings, which are fabric-covered. Pither drew on his experience as a professional cyclist and cycle manufacturer to build the aircraft, and in doing so tackled and beat the problem of how to keep the aircraft light enough to be lifted by the power of the engines that were available.

Apparently the resemblance of both Pither's engine and his aircraft design to the experimental 1910 JAP motor and aircraft design built in England remains a mystery. Why were these two aircraft so similar? Maybe that's where common design thoughts had progressed to. In my experience, it is not unlikely for designers and manufacturers to reach similar concepts at the same time in the evolution of a product.

Pither also designed and built his own car, and built petrol-driven motors for boats and agricultural machinery. He was obviously quite a pioneering engineer.

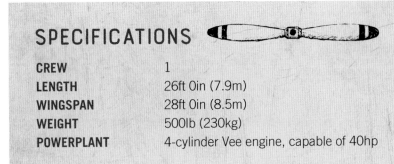

SPECIFICATIONS

CREW	1
LENGTH	26ft 0in (7.9m)
WINGSPAN	28ft 0in (8.5m)
WEIGHT	500lb (230kg)
POWERPLANT	4-cylinder Vee engine, capable of 40hp

The replica has flown successfully at a height of about 14 feet. The warped-wing configuration makes turning a little problematic, so she is generally kept to straight takeoff, flight and landings. Control in the air is by a pedal-operated rudder, and lateral stability is generally achieved by warping the rear edges of the wings, controlled by a steering wheel. Pitch control is lever-operated, and the undercarriage is bicycle wheels fitted with shock absorbers.

Pither's claim to have flown on Oreti Beach on 5 July 1910 relies entirely on his own description of the experience as reported in the *Southland Daily News*. Other flights have believed to have taken place. There is no doubt that if the replica is an accurate reincarnation, then the original Pither could have indeed achieved controlled flight.

Walking around this aircraft, one realises how quickly aircraft design evolved. From these early attempts in 1910, in just another 33 years the first jet-fighters would be flying.

AIRCRAFT OF THE GREAT WAR

My first introduction to aircraft of the Great War came in 1957, as a seven-year-old, when I discovered the Biggles books by Captain W.E. Johns. For those of you unfamiliar with the Biggles books, they were *Boy's Own* type books written about a fictional fighter pilot of World War I by the name of James 'Biggles' Bigglesworth. I don't remember a lot about the books after nearly 60 years, but I do know I was besotted with them and devoured them for a year or two at the rate of about one a week. I can remember Biggles had some close mates, Algy, Ginger and Bertie, who wore a monocle when not flying. These characters featured in all of the books. I think they flew Sopwith Camels, and their arch nemesis was a Captain von Stalin. The author himself had been a World War I fighter pilot. The next introduction was the mid-1960s movie *The Blue Max*, a World War I drama told from the German side. This was followed in the 1970s by a television series called *Wings*, which followed the lives of three English World War I fighter pilots. After that, I read *Aces High* and *High Road to China*, both great books, with the latter being made into an equally good film. With each of these movies and books, I was totally enthralled and transported back emotionally to another time and another place. For some reason, these old aircraft seem to exert an emotional hook that absolutely draws me in.

Back in 1995, an incident caused me to research the early days of the command by Manfred von Richthofen (the Red Baron) of what became the famous Jasta 11 group. Again, the exploits of these pilots enthralled me, except that this time it was all true.

The triumphs and tragedies, and the bravery, of the pilots who flew these fragile and sometimes unreliable flying machines, day after day, trying to shoot each other down, made for amazing reading. With each 1000 feet they climbed, the air temperature dropped 4 degrees, so at 10,000 feet it was 40 degrees colder than the land-based temperature. Something you don't think about. It must have been mind-numbingly cold at that height in the open cockpits, yet here were these pilots, nursing their engines, often having to pressure their oil, operate their guns, wipe the oil spray from their goggles, and fly the planes in almost aerobatic flight as they engaged in their dogfights.

To be able to write this book and include flying examples, and one static example, of these magnificent World War I fighter aircraft has been a real highlight for me. To find the Bristol Scout replica built by Jack Godfrey, a Hamilton pensioner in his eighties, at a Hamilton retirement village, and Graham Orphan's Fokker Triplane and Nieuport 11 at Blenheim, was great. Then to find people like Sir Peter Jackson, who has the passion and fascination with World War I aircraft, and the means to bring them alive and recreate aviation history, is fantastic. To see the impressive and talented people, like Gene De Marco and his crew, whom Peter has gathered around him, restore and recreate authentic reproductions of these old aircraft is awesome. Then to watch Gene and a small band of experienced pilots fly these machines is like a dream come true. They bring back my boyhood memories of Biggles, and the movies I saw and the books I have read.

This collection is not only world-class, but it is probably the largest and most diversified World War I collection in the world. We, as a nation, should thank our lucky stars that Sir Peter Jackson is prepared to share his wonderful collection with us, and add to New Zealand's enviable reputation of vintage and iconic aircraft. If you have not seen these wonderful World War I aircraft flying, then add it to your bucket list. It is a must-do!

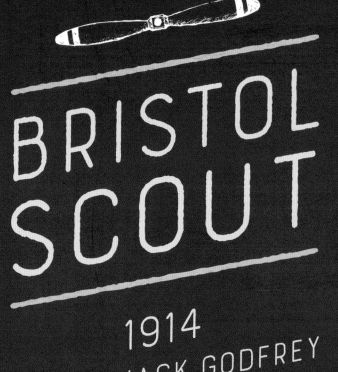

BRISTOL SCOUT

1914

BUILT BY JACK GODFREY

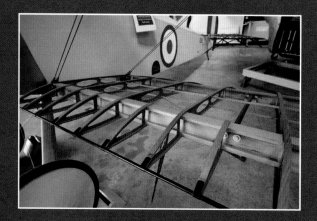

The Bristol Scout biplane, first designed in 1913 and produced in 1914, was a light forward staggerwing biplane, designed for racing. The first one was powered by an 80hp Gnome Lambda rotary engine, and fitted with an enclosed cowling. The first flight was in February 1914. She achieved a speed of 97.5mph in her trial flight. The second and third Scouts were fitted with 80hp Le Rhône 9C rotary engines.

Impressed with the Scout, the War Office ordered 12. The production aircraft differed slightly in build from their predecessors, and marked the beginning of the fighter aircraft, as distinct from reconnaissance aircraft being retro-fitted with machine guns. At the time, synchronised machine guns firing through the propeller hadn't happened. The Scout was fitted with a single machine gun mounted on the left-hand side of the fuselage and offset to fire forward on an angle so as to clear the propeller. Some of the Royal Navy Air Services Scouts had the machine gun fitted to the top wing, giving more accurate fire in the actual direction in which the aircraft was flying.

The example shown here is a replica aircraft and is domiciled at the Classic Flyers Museum at Mount Maunganui. As can be seen from the photographs, she is a static aircraft, with two-thirds of her wearing the fabric covering, and the remaining third uncovered, showing the wooden framework of the wing and tail. The workmanship is exquisite. The cowling is aluminium, with a wooden extension bodywork back to the cockpit on the top third of the fuselage.

The amazing thing about this aircraft is that it was researched and built in a small communal garage at Alandale Retirement Village in Hamilton by retiree Jack Godfrey. He spent countless hours working on the aircraft over an 18-month period. He just loves being in the workshop, and, when the Scout was done with, he started on a metre-long scale version of an SE5a biplane. As Jack said, 'I don't want to play bowls or snooker; I prefer to be here making things, and it gets me out of my wife's hair.'

Jack is one of Nature's true gentlemen and quite a character. All of his life he has been interested in aircraft, making models since he was a nipper. As a teenager he wanted to be an aircraft engineer, and hung around the Hastings aerodrome, helping out on the aero club's Tiger Moths. Jack even got a scholarship to learn to fly. He got his first flight, but then his parents found out and put a stop to it. So instead he did a printing apprenticeship, but many years later, in Hamilton, found himself working for Aero Chrome Plate as a cylinder-grinder operator. Being a clever guy, he tinkered with and adjusted the grinding machine, managing to up the machine's output from 8–10 cylinders a day to 18–20 cylinders a day. These had to be machined to very fine tolerances, and the finish had to be perfect. When the Hamilton aero companies amalgamated, Jack was asked to do a stocktake of parts, and, as a result of a job well done, ended up as their purchasing officer for all overseas parts. By this stage, Jack had built himself a Jodel aircraft from scratch. It took him six years part-time to build, before on-selling her a year after she first flew. Part of the deal was that he could still go flying in her.

Talking to the Cambridge Armistice chairman one day about the cost of air displays, Jack said, 'I could build you a replica aircraft for less than that.' Cambridge Armistice paid for the materials, and 2000 hours later Jack had produced what you see today. He took a three-dimensional drawing at 1/140th scale and scaled it up to 1/120th scale. From there he scaled it up to full size. He used western hemlock for the frame, as it has similar properties to spruce, which is the wood used in the original aircraft. Using modern glues and laser technology on the wing spars, he created a near-similar frame of exact proportions. He calls her a non-authentic replica with the exact proportions of the original plane. 'Really, I built it just like a large model aeroplane. Unfortunately, the budget could not stretch to a motor. The propeller was hand-carved by a friend, Bas McCarn, with Gene De Marco supplying the cane cockpit chair.' Not bad for a young lad in his early eighties. Jack showed me some photographs of large-model aeroplanes and a flying model of a Westpac helicopter that he had built for Westpac. He still builds model aircraft of quite large proportions; one of them is a scale version of a 1910 aircraft. Like his Bristol Scout, the workmanship is absolutely exquisite.

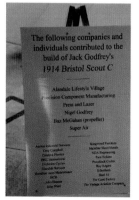

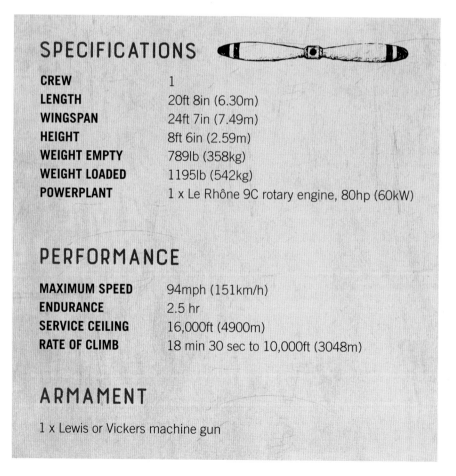

SPECIFICATIONS

CREW	1
LENGTH	20ft 8in (6.30m)
WINGSPAN	24ft 7in (7.49m)
HEIGHT	8ft 6in (2.59m)
WEIGHT EMPTY	789lb (358kg)
WEIGHT LOADED	1195lb (542kg)
POWERPLANT	1 x Le Rhône 9C rotary engine, 80hp (60kW)

PERFORMANCE

MAXIMUM SPEED	94mph (151km/h)
ENDURANCE	2.5 hr
SERVICE CEILING	16,000ft (4900m)
RATE OF CLIMB	18 min 30 sec to 10,000ft (3048m)

ARMAMENT

1 x Lewis or Vickers machine gun

THE VINTAGE AVIATOR LTD (TVAL)

Most of the World War I collection of aircraft you are soon to read about, and admire the amazing photographs of, could not have been written about, or even conceived of, but for the amazing work of The Vintage Aviator Ltd. If this company had not been formed, and had not then restored and reproduced these incredible aircraft, this would be a slim volume of work on World War I aircraft, especially on airworthy examples. There would have been very few other World War I planes to talk about or photograph, let alone witness flying in New Zealand. This company has, alone, restored and re-created many aircraft, both flying examples and museum statics, of which just 14 airworthy examples are showcased in this book. The restorations of the old originals are superb, but the re-creations are something else again. The words 'retro' or 'replica' don't even come close to describing these aircraft, as that is not what they are. The terms 're-creation aircraft' or 'reproduction aircraft', although strictly true, do not really cut the mustard, either.

On TVAL's comprehensive website, I discovered the mammoth amount of research they have undertaken before each build proceeds. And when I read Gene De Marco's accounts of each build, not only of the aircraft, but in most cases of the engines and ancillary parts as well, I began to have a small appreciation of the very high level of skill and craftsmanship applied to each aircraft. When I read further, and discovered the modern technology applied to the manufacture of these aircraft, and in some cases the reverse-engineering that has taken place, I realised that the integrity and authenticity of the builds are probably better than the original aircraft built back in the 1913–1918 era. Even the replicas that have been imported have received a high-class going-over and been TVALed.

As a former production manager of many years' standing, managing a large caravan, motorhome, boat and transportable-building company, I can truly understand the production process, from plan to manufacture to completion. Quite frankly, I am in awe of what Gene De Marco and his crew at The Vintage Aviator Ltd have achieved. The best compliment to pay them that I can think of is to call their aircraft 'modern-day factory-produced authentic originals'. The extreme efforts they have gone to in search of perfection is just amazing. To achieve that level in the build, as they have done with each aircraft, is truly superb.

For any reader who has a bent towards, or an interest in, the technical or production side of these aircraft, then I would highly recommend spending a lot of time on their website. Similarly, if it's the flying of these machines that interests you, then some of Gene's stories of the test-flights are equally as fascinating.

A big thank-you to Sir Peter Jackson, Gene De Marco and their crew at The Vintage Aviator, for bringing back to life these amazing and iconic heritage aircraft.

BE.2c

1914 (TVAL)

The BE.2 came in a number of variants. The layperson would not really notice any difference between these variants, and in some cases even the current-day experts would have to look hard. This featured aircraft is one of TVAL's wonderful reproductions. Having access to many of the plans, and also with a BE.2 actual restoration to use as reference, the team was able to re-create an aircraft that is correct in every detail, right to the specifications of the variant 'c'. The livery is as it was in 1914. Note the Union Jack on the wings. This was the correct format until December 1914, when the roundels replaced the Union Jack. This aircraft is powered by an original Renault 80hp engine. For the technically-minded reader, there is a lot of very interesting information on the TVAL website regarding the BE.2 aircraft models.

So for a little history on the BE.2c. The BE.2 was a British-designed two-seater biplane. They were in service with the Royal Flying Corps (RFC) from 1912 to the end of World War I. Around 3500 were built. Initially, they were designed as a very stable aircraft specifically for reconnaissance. At that period, aircraft were considered only good for reporting enemy troop movements to the ground forces. No one had really considered aerial warfare.

The BE.2c had the biggest changes in design from the earlier BE.2b. It has the same fuselage as the 'b', but otherwise was really a new type. They were powered by a more powerful Renault 80hp engine. The wings were staggered, and for the first time had ailerons rather than the old wing-warping style of the BE.2b. Normally the aircraft were armed with a camera, but, with their emerging role as a light bomber, they were often retro-fitted with a machine-gun mount. Often these were rigged by the ground crews of a particular squadron.

Their slow performance and lack of manoeuvrability earned them the British nickname of 'Fokker fodder'. The Germans called them *kaltes Fleisch* (cold meat). Later in the war, as more sophisticated fighters took the war to the Germans, the old BE.2c found her destruction rates dropping. I guess the Germans had their hands full with the superior fighters coming at them and engaging them.

An incident illustrating the popularity of the BE.2s, and the poor training of new pilots, took place in France in 1917, when six pilots, newly arrived and not yet allocated to a squadron, were given the task of ferrying BE.2s between RFC depots at Saint-Omer and Candas. One crashed in transit, three crashed on landing, one went missing (the pilot was killed), and the last one arrived safely.

The BE.2c was manufactured by a number of companies in England, and when TVAL came to build this aircraft they were able to gather together a number of original plans from a number of manufacturers. These were all cross-referenced before the build. TVAL has made a great job of reproducing this aircraft, and, as I walked around her, I was once again reminded of just how the design of aircraft matured at an incredible rate over a very short period of time. This early aircraft was built of wood and fabric and wire. One is reminded of an extremely complicated, very large, motorised kite. That may be being unkind to her, but every time I look at the photographs of a BE.2c, the same feelings remain.

It is a very cool feeling to walk around these early aircraft, and I find it visually exciting to gaze upon them and just take in the look, the design and the detail. Sometimes I just shake my head in wonderment. I am so glad that TVAL are recreating and restoring such wonderful iconic aircraft, which would otherwise be lost in history books forever. They are truly bringing history alive.

SPECIFICATIONS

CREW	2 (pilot and observer)
LENGTH	27ft 3in (8.31m)
WINGSPAN	37ft 0in (11.28m)
HEIGHT	11ft 1½in (3.39m)
WEIGHT EMPTY	1370lb (623kg)
WEIGHT LOADED	2350lb (1068kg)
POWERPLANT	1 x RAF 1a aircooled engine, 90hp (66kW) (other engines also used, notably the Renault 80hp engine)

PERFORMANCE

MAXIMUM SPEED	72mph (116km/h)
ENDURANCE	3 hr 15 min
SERVICE CEILING	10,000ft (3050m)
RATE OF CLIMB	6 min 30 sec to 3500ft (1070m)
	45 min 15 sec to 10,000ft (3050m)

ARMAMENT

GUNS	1 x .303 (7.7mm) Lewis gun for observer
BOMBS	224lb (100kg) of bombs

AVRO 504K
1915 (TVAL)

The Avro 504 was first designed in 1913, and flew in September of that year. The 'K' variant appeared around 1915. The first of the 504 versions were initially sold to the Royal Flying Corps (RFC) and the Royal Navy Air Service (RNAS) in the same year. During the war they were initially used as frontline fighters, but quickly became outdated. An Avro 504 was the first Allied plane to be shot down. Where they became outstanding was as trainers. Production quickly ramped up with the 'J' variant and, with the 'K' variant, they became the first planes in Britain to be mass-produced. The 'K' series had modified engine bearers to accept a range of different motors, as a single engine supply could not keep up with production. The Avro was a two-seater. By 1918, 8340 Avro 504s had been built. Most were powered by the 100hp (75kW) Gnome rotary engine or the 110hp (82kW) Le Rhône rotary engine.

After the war, the RFC, now under the guise of the Royal Air Force (RAF), continued to use the Avro 504K as a trainer for quite a number of years. They were also exported in numbers, with countries such as Russia, China, Belgium, Brazil, Chile, Denmark, Greece, Thailand, South Africa, Australia and New Zealand receiving them. Denmark, Belgium, Canada, Japan and Australia also built them under licence.

The 504K featured here is a restoration of an original by The Vintage Aviator Ltd in New Zealand. It is a stunning restoration, and looks like a new original aircraft. I had the opportunity to get up close to this aircraft and to watch her fly. To hear the clatter of the rotary engine, listen to it cut out, and then clatter away again mid-flight brings home the level of engineering of the time and how flimsy these aircraft were, and also how things have progressed through the years. To walk around this aircraft and look at the fabric covering not only the wings, but also the fuselage, just reinforces that feeling of flimsiness.

The landings of these aircraft always fascinate me. The rotary engine always gives them the tendency to want to go to the right. The large biplane wings give the aircraft extraordinary lift, and, as speed drifts off, so does directional stability, because of the size of the tail fin. So landing is a combination of backing off the power, but blipping the throttle to keep up enough speed to maintain directional stability, while trying to touch down an aircraft that would rather stay in the air. If you get the opportunity, really watch the landings of these Great War aircraft. I suspect the landing is the most skilful part of piloting them.

SPECIFICATIONS

CREW	2
LENGTH	29ft 5in (8.97m)
WINGSPAN	36ft 0in (10.97m)
HEIGHT	10ft 5in (3.18m)
WING AREA	330sqft (30.7sqm)
WEIGHT EMPTY	1231lb (558kg)
WEIGHT LOADED	1829lb (830kg)
POWERPLANT	1 x Le Rhône 9J rotary, 110hp (82kW)
	or 1 x Gnome rotary, 100hp (75kW)

PERFORMANCE

MAXIMUM SPEED	90mph (145km/h)
CRUISE SPEED	75mph (121km/h)
RANGE	250 miles (402km)
SERVICE CEILING	16,000ft (4876m)
RATE OF CLIMB	3500ft (1065m) in 5 min

ARMAMENT

1 x fixed .303 Lewis machine gun in top wing

This FE2b-1 (known as the 'Fee') has been painted up to replicate an actual Fee that served in the Great War. She represents an aircraft flown by Captain Douglas Grinnell-Milne and observer/gunner Corporal D. MacMaster of the Royal Flying Corps. The original Fee was one of four presentation machines gifted to 25 Squadron, and is marked with her benefactor, the Government of Zanzibar, on the port side. The squadron was formed in Scotland, so the aircraft was called *The Scotch Express*.

The Fee apparently was a very stable aircraft to fly, and in formation presented an awful lot of firepower. However, they were pretty slow, and, while they were pretty good in 1916, by the early 1917 they were hopelessly out-of-date and outclassed by the new wave of fighters. The base of the cockpit had a steel plate lining it, which gave the crew a little protection when doing camera work. One of the Fee's roles was to fly low over the German lines and photograph enemy positions. At a height of 200 feet, and moving probably at 70mph, they would have made a pretty tempting target. The Fees were also successfully used as bombers on night missions.

The FE2b-1 was powered by a Beardmore 160hp engine, or a 120hp engine, but sometimes by an RAF5a or a Rolls Royce Eagle engine. When it came to TVAL recreating this FE2b-1, they really had a choice of engines, but, as luck would have it, they were offered a 160hp Beardmore that had actually come out of a FE2b-1!

A total of 1939 FE2bs were built. Today, only one survives, as a static display in the Royal Air Force museum in London, and even that is in equal parts original and re-creation: the nacelle and engine are original, while the rest has been re-created.

This example is fully airworthy. Gene's story of actually flying this machine is highly illuminating and totally fascinating. It is well worth hitting the website and becoming immersed. Two other re-creations have been built by TVAL, one for static display and another flying version like the one we have written about here.

SPECIFICATIONS

CREW	2
LENGTH	32ft 3in (9.83m)
WINGSPAN	47ft 9in (14.55m)
HEIGHT	12ft 8in (3.85m)
WEIGHT EMPTY	2061lb (937kg)
WEIGHT LOADED	3037lb (1380kg)
POWERPLANT	1 x Beardmore 6-cylinder inline piston engine, 160hp (119kW)

PERFORMANCE

MAXIMUM SPEED	91.5mph (147km/h)
ENDURANCE	3 hr
SERVICE CEILING	11,000ft (3353m)
RATE OF CLIMB	39 min 44 sec to 10,000ft (3048m)

ARMAMENT

1 or 2 x .303in (7.7mm) Lewis gun for observer (1 mounted in front and 1 firing back over top wing)

NIEUPORT 11

1915 (TVAL)

The Nieuport Aeronautical Company was a French company, and, prior to World War I, Nieuport chief designer Gustave Delage began designing a new biplane to compete in the famous Gordon Bennett Trophy Race. With France's commitment to the war, Nieuport didn't compete in the race, and the little biplane (the Nieuport 10) was reconfigured for military use. She was nicknamed '*Bebe*' ('Baby', in English). In the military version, she was known as the 'Nieuport 11', and became a single-seater fighter. *Bebe* models were highly manoeuvrable, and through 1916 worked well as an effective fighter plane. They were powered by a front-mounted Le Rhône 9C (9-cylinder) aircooled rotary piston engine running a two-blade propeller. Armament was a single Lewis or Hotchkiss .303 calibre (7.7mm) machine gun mounted to the top wing.

The Nieuport 11 was first seen operationally at the Front at the beginning of 1916. Italy also produced Nieuport 11s under licence, with some 646 being built by the Italians. They were officially retired from active frontline service at the end of summer 1917, having by that time become outdated. Overall, some 7200 examples were built.

The flying example seen here was originally built as an exact replica in the 1960s in California. The livery represents an actual Nieuport that flew in the Great War, and is based on one of the aircraft that flew in 80 Squadron in the Italian Air Force. The character depicted on the fuselage was known as 'Fortunello', from the popular comic-strip of the time 'The Happy Hooligan'. Fortunello means 'lucky'. The little Nieuport carries an original Le Rhône 80hp rotary engine.

This aircraft captures the essence of her era perfectly, and is a joy to watch flying. I saw this little plane being fired up, and watched in fascination as Gene De Marco listened to the engine. He had it shut down, dashed off to the engineering hangar, and came back and changed the spark-plug in one cylinder. Firing it up again, he listened to it for a while, then gave the pilot the thumbs-up. Off she went, performing faultlessly. Gene has obviously developed an engineer's ear, just knowing by the sound what a problem might be, and knowing when the engine is on song. I have only ever seen one other man who could do that to the same extent, and that was with highly-tuned racing-car engines.

SPECIFICATIONS

CREW	1
LENGTH	19ft (5.8m)
WINGSPAN	24ft 9in (7.55m)
HEIGHT	7ft 10½in (2.4m)
WING AREA	140sqft (13sqm)
WEIGHT EMPTY	759lb (344kg)
WEIGHT LOADED	1058lb (480kg)
POWERPLANT	1 x Le Rhône 9-cylinder aircooled rotary engine, 80hp (60kW)

PERFORMANCE

MAXIMUM SPEED	97mph (156km/h)
RANGE	205 miles (330km)
SERVICE CEILING	15,090ft (4600m)
RATE OF CLIMB	15 min to 9840ft (3000m)

ARMAMENT

1 x machine gun (either a Lewis or a Hotchkiss)

SOPWITH PUP (TVAL)

1916

The Sopwith Pup entered service with the Royal Flying Corps and the Royal Navy Air Service (RNAS) in autumn 1916. After a year's service they were relegated to home defence and training, simply because ongoing developments of aircraft design outdated them. In the war, performance was everything, and as newer aircraft on both sides appeared with superior performance and armaments, it simply became suicide to continue operating an outdated aircraft.

The Pup, however, was apparently a lovely aircraft to fly. She was fully aerobatic up to 15,000 feet. Most of the production Pups were powered by an 80hp (60kW) Le Rhône 9-cylinder rotary engine. The Pup's light weight and generous wing area gave her a good rate of climb, and being highly manoeuvrable could easily out-turn the German Albatros.

The Sopwith Pup was officially named the 'Sopwith Scout'. The 'Pup' nickname came about because pilots thought it to be the pup of the larger Sopwith 1½ Strutter. The name was frowned upon, but 'Pup' stuck, and Sopwith went on to name many of their aircraft after animals.

A Sopwith Pup was the first aircraft to land on a moving carrier ship. This tricky landing was carried out by RNAS pilot Squadron Commander E.H. Dunning in early August 1917.

The Pups were armed with a single Vickers .303 synchronised machine gun mounted on the top of the fuselage.

A total of 1770 Sopwith Pups were produced. There are three known original Pups that have survived, along with a Sopwith Dove that was converted to a Pup configuration in the 1930s. TVAL have built two stunning reproductions, both running original Le Rhône engines. Both are airworthy.

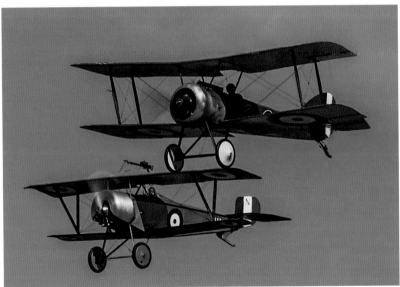

SPECIFICATIONS

CREW	1
LENGTH	19ft 3¾in (5.89m)
WINGSPAN	26ft 6in (8.08m)
HEIGHT	9ft 5in (2.87m)
WEIGHT EMPTY	787lb (358kg)
WEIGHT LOADED	1225lb (557kg)
POWERPLANT	1 x Le Rhône aircooled rotary engine, 80hp (60kW)

PERFORMANCE

MAXIMUM SPEED	111mph (180km/h)
ENDURANCE	3 hr
SERVICE CEILING	17,000ft (5600m)
RATE OF CLIMB	14 min to 10,000ft (3050m)
	35 min to 16,100ft (4910m)

ARMAMENT

1 x .303in (7.7mm) Vickers synchronised forward-firing machine gun

AIRCO DH.5

1917 (TVAL)

This aircraft made me do a double-take. I have come across aircraft with staggered wings in my recent aeronautical travels, but this staggered wing was not in the usual configuration. Normally a staggered wing would have the top wing stepped forward with the pilot's cockpit aft of the wing. The Airco DH.5 has a reverse configuration, with the top wing stepped further to the rear than the lower wing. Termed a 'negative stagger', it placed the cockpit in front of the top wing. This afforded the pilot unobstructed views to the front of the aircraft without having to peer around the top wing. This is what it was designed for, and it fulfilled the task admirably. Unfortunately, there was one major flaw with the design, and it was a lethal one. It created a massive blindspot to the rear of the aircraft. The pilot could not see behind him at all, and, as most fighter pilots tried to attack from behind, to avoid his opponents' guns, it made the Airco DH.5 pilots particularly vulnerable.

The plane became unpopular with pilots, and really was inferior to the earlier Sopwith Pup, and became even more inferior with the introduction of the Sopwith Camel and the SE5a. As a fighter, they really didn't make the grade, but with the fantastic forward view they excelled as a 'ground attack' aircraft for strafing troops and trenches. By January 1918, they had disappeared from frontline service.

The featured Airco DH.5 is owned by the Vintage Aviation Heritage Trust, and is a full-scale reproduction built in the United States by John Shiveley. She is fully airworthy and flies in New Zealand vintage World War I fighter shows. There are no original surviving DH.5s left in the world. On arrival in New Zealand, she was restored by The Vintage Aviator Ltd.

We saw and photographed the Airco DH.5 at a flying weekend at Masterton's Hood Aerodrome, and I was able to talk to the pilot. I had noticed that before he took off he had had a long conversation with Gene De Marco. Gene is a highly qualified aeronautical engineer, and heads up the team at The Vintage Aviator Ltd. He is also their chief test pilot, and has probably racked up more flying hours on World War I fighters — both restored originals and reproduction models — than anyone else in the world. In talking to the pilot, I discovered that this was the first time he had flown such a craft, and he had been invited by Gene to fly the Airco DH.5. He had been very appreciative of Gene's advice, and was fair buzzing with excitement when he landed. The pilot's name is Dan Pezaro, and in everyday life he is a flight lieutenant in the Royal New Zealand Air Force in command of an Iroquois helicopter. It is amazing how many professional pilots I have met who in their leisure time fly a vintage aircraft for the pure pleasure and joy of doing so. Such people are not just pilots, they are airmen and -women in the truest sense of the word. They just love flying and being airborne!

SPECIFICATIONS

CREW	1
LENGTH	22ft (6.71m)
WINGSPAN	25ft 8in (7.83m)
HEIGHT	9ft 1½in (2.78m)
WING AREA	212.1sqft (19.7sqm)
WEIGHT EMPTY	1010lb (459kg)
WEIGHT LOADED	1492lb (676kg)
POWERPLANT	1 x Le Rhône 9J 9-cylinder rotary engine, 110hp (82kW)

PERFORMANCE

MAXIMUM SPEED	102mph (164km/h)
ENDURANCE	2 hr 45 min
SERVICE CEILING	16,000ft (4878m)
RATE OF CLIMB	12 min 25 sec to 10,000ft (3050m)

ARMAMENT

GUNS	1 x .303in (7.7mm) Vickers machine gun
BOMBS	Racks for 4 x 25lb (10kg) bombs under fuselage

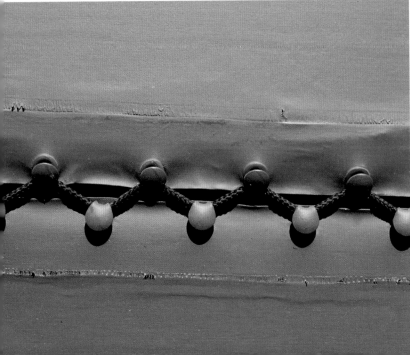

SE5a

1917 (TVAL)

'What an ugly-looking boxy front that aircraft has on it.' That was my first impression of the SE5a reproduction aircraft I saw at Hood Aerodrome. My second thought was that 'with the aerodynamics of a flying box, she must handle like a pig'. I thought that the Sopwith Camel was a much more aerodynamic shape and altogether a prettier plane. Well, how wrong could I be? The Sopwith Camel was apparently quite difficult to fly, and killed as many pilots in crashes as were actually shot down by the Germans. The SE5a, on the other hand, was beautiful to fly, easy to take off and land, and was stable in-flight, making them a great gun platform, thus allowing pilots to fire from a greater distance. For what they lacked in agility and manoeuvrability in comparison to the Camel, they more than made up for it in sheer speed. With a maximum level-flight speed of 138mph, they could outrun every other fighter on the Western Front. They were strongly built, and could withstand speeds of over 200mph in a steep dive. Added to that, their gentle manners and their aforementioned characteristics gave new pilots a much higher chance of surviving their first few weeks at the Front. Many of the new pilots were posted to active service squadrons with only 20 hours' total flying time, half of which was probably solo time!

The SE5 entered service in April 1917 powered by a 150hp Hispano-Suiza engine. They were underpowered and unreliable. An upgraded 200hp Hispano-Suiza engine was fitted, along with other engines modified by an English company and called the Wolseley Viper. These modified units came out with the designation 'SE5a', and proved to be one of the Allies' great fighter planes. The SE5a had a distinguished career in the hands of the British, American, Canadian and Australian forces. Our own New Zealand hero, Major Keith 'Grid' Caldwell (25 aerial victories), flew a SE5a.

The total production figures were in excess of 5200 units. Just six original SE5s are known to have survived, but a number of fine reproductions have been built, including four completely authentic reproductions built by The Vintage Aviator Ltd in New Zealand. Three of these are airworthy, including the SE5a featured in these photographs. The other is a non-airworthy, but accurate reproduction in the Omaka Aviation Heritage Centre, depicting the famous incident where 'Grid' Caldwell managed to stabilise his SE5a after an airborne collision by standing on the wing and flying back to land.

A lot of information was available with regards to the plans and specifications of the SE5a, so the team at The Vintage Aviator have been able to recreate exceptionally authentic reproductions right down to making replica machine guns. However, they were a complex and difficult plane to build, and the team had to overcome many challenges along the way. Much credit must go to them, though, because the workmanship and authentic detail is just stunning. These reproductions are brilliant in every way, and they display the same flying traits as the originals. Like all of the World War I New Zealand fighter collection, the SE5a's are a pure joy to watch in flight.

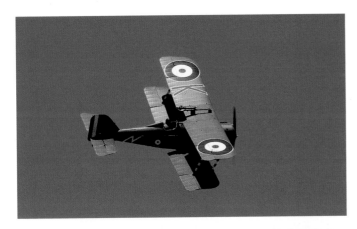

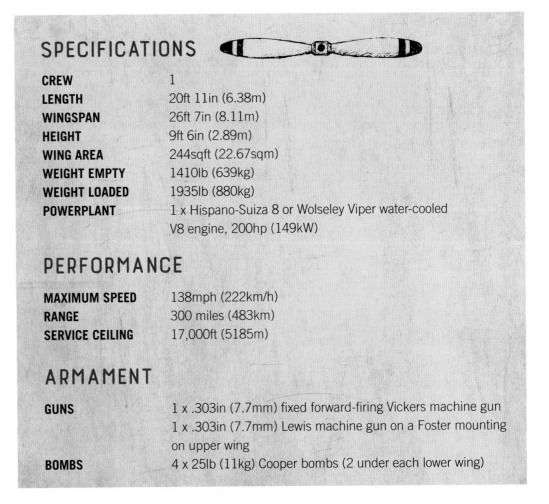

SPECIFICATIONS

CREW	1
LENGTH	20ft 11in (6.38m)
WINGSPAN	26ft 7in (8.11m)
HEIGHT	9ft 6in (2.89m)
WING AREA	244sqft (22.67sqm)
WEIGHT EMPTY	1410lb (639kg)
WEIGHT LOADED	1935lb (880kg)
POWERPLANT	1 x Hispano-Suiza 8 or Wolseley Viper water-cooled V8 engine, 200hp (149kW)

PERFORMANCE

MAXIMUM SPEED	138mph (222km/h)
RANGE	300 miles (483km)
SERVICE CEILING	17,000ft (5185m)

ARMAMENT

GUNS	1 x .303in (7.7mm) fixed forward-firing Vickers machine gun 1 x .303in (7.7mm) Lewis machine gun on a Foster mounting on upper wing
BOMBS	4 x 25lb (11kg) Cooper bombs (2 under each lower wing)

SOPWITH TRIPLANE

1917 (TVAL)

The Sopwith Triplane was designed and built shortly after the Sopwith Pup in 1916. The prototype, flown by Sopwith's chief test pilot, Harry Hawker, surprised all of the onlookers when after 15 minutes' flying time he did three successive loops in her.

With the test being a success, the Royal Navy Air Service (RNAS) ordered a number of them. They appeared at the Front in February through to May 1917. The three-wing configuration gave them great climbing ability, and they were highly manoeuvrable, giving them an advantage over the German's famous Albatros DIII. They also had a better outright speed advantage over the Germans. Affectionally known as the 'Tripehound', or even just as the 'Tripe', she shone for a short time, particularly with RNAS 10 Squadron. In three months, 10 Squadron's B Flight (better known as the 'Black Flight') accounted for 87 German aircraft. This all-Canadian flight, distinguishable by their black-painted fins and cowlings, named their individual planes *Black Maria*, *Black Prince*, *Black George*, *Black Death* and *Black Sheep*.

Their success sent the Germans into a design frenzy, trying to emulate the Tripe. Over 34 different triplane prototypes were produced by German manufacturers, with what became known as the Fokker Dr.1 Triplane going into production as the German's answer to the British threat.

Unbeknown to the Germans, problems started to arise with the Sopwith Triplane. When damaged, because of the way they were built, they were very difficult to repair and had to be sent back to a more extensive repair facility behind the lines. This caused delays at the Front. Spare parts became difficult to obtain, and some suffered wing collapses in steep dives. Only 147 had been built, and with the arrival of the Sopwith Camel, which outclassed it in every respect, they were soon retired from frontline duties. Another drawback had been her armament, carrying only one machine gun, whereas most German planes carried two. The Tripe aircraft were powered by an 130hp Clerget 9B rotary engine.

The featured replica Triplane has been painted up in the colours of RNAS 10 Squadron's B Flight, and wears the name *Black Maria*. The Vintage Aviator Ltd not only builds authentic originals from scratch, it also restores originals and takes on other projects. This replica comes under 'Other Projects'. This particular Sopwith Triplane replica was started by a chap called Chad Wille from Corning, Iowa, in the United States. Working from original drawings, but using modern simplified construction techniques, Chad built the fuselage frame out of steel tube, and simplified the wing construction. Chad has built a number of Triplanes, but TVAL became involved in this one, receiving a fuselage and tail assembly that was basically complete. The build was carried on from there, with TVAL adding their own ideas, bringing the aircraft as near as possible to a correct look. Although there are more modern, better-lasting fabrics now available, TVAL rejected them and opted for the traditional Irish linen for the covering material. This enabled them to get much closer to the original look by being able to maintain the clear 'doped' (stained) undersides of the original colour scheme, which added some authenticity to the look of the aircraft. As is usual with anything that TVAL tackles, much attention was paid to detail, even down to a correct replica machine gun which was designed and constructed in-house. The exterior colour scheme and name, mentioned earlier, replicated the aircraft of Canadian flying ace Raymond Collishaw. While not an authentic reproduction or an original restoration, this replica is pretty accurate in appearance, flies like the original, and looks very close to the original. As one would expect, the workmanship is of an exceptionally high standard.

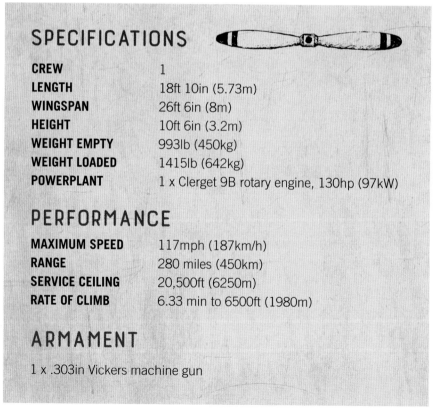

SPECIFICATIONS

CREW	1
LENGTH	18ft 10in (5.73m)
WINGSPAN	26ft 6in (8m)
HEIGHT	10ft 6in (3.2m)
WEIGHT EMPTY	993lb (450kg)
WEIGHT LOADED	1415lb (642kg)
POWERPLANT	1 x Clerget 9B rotary engine, 130hp (97kW)

PERFORMANCE

MAXIMUM SPEED	117mph (187km/h)
RANGE	280 miles (450km)
SERVICE CEILING	20,500ft (6250m)
RATE OF CLIMB	6.33 min to 6500ft (1980m)

ARMAMENT

1 x .303in Vickers machine gun

SOPWITH CAMEL F.1

1917 (TVAL)

The Sopwith Camel F.1 is probably, along with the Fokker Triplane, the best-known World War I aircraft. For those who have only a passing interest in aviation, these two planes will be remembered from the Snoopy versus the Red Baron comic strips, and The Royal Guardsmen's hit song 'Snoopy's Christmas'.

The British Sopwith Camel was introduced to the Western Front in 1917. They superseded the Sopwith Pup and the Sopwith Triplane in an effort to overcome the Germans' air superiority. Although there were similarities between the Pup and the Camel, the latter was bigger, more bulky in the fuselage, and carried a more powerful rotary engine. They also carried twin synchronised machine guns. These guns carried a metal fairing over the gun breeches, designed to protect the guns from freezing-over at high altitudes. It was from this feature that the Sopwith F.1 became nicknamed and universally known as the 'Camel', although 'Camel' was never part of her official designation.

The handling characteristics of the Camel were difficult, with the large rotary engine, the fuel tank, guns and pilot all situated in the first 7 feet of the aircraft. (This made up some 90 per cent of the Camel's weight.) Add to that the strong gyroscopic effect of the engine, and a full load of fuel, which changed the centre of gravity, and in the hands of a novice pilot you had a potentially lethal combination. It is often quoted that more pilots were killed by the Camel in takeoff than were killed by the enemy. True or false? I am not sure, but it makes for an intriguing legend. Despite this, the Camel was highly manoeuvrable, especially to the right, using the gyroscopic effect of the engine. In the hands of experienced pilots, she helped turn the tide against German air superiority. The pilots would joke that the Camel offered the choices between 'a wooden cross, the Red Cross or a Victoria Cross'. The Sopwith Camel F.1 was credited with shooting down 1294 enemy aircraft, making her the most effective Allied fighter in the Great War.

There are known to be just eight original survivors in the world. There is a restored example (Camel F.1 *B5747*) in a museum in Brussels, and another (Camel F.1 *B7280*) in a museum in Poland. Restoration began on this one in 2007, and was completed in 2010. Yet another (Camel 2F.1 *N6812*) is in the Imperial War Museum in London. The Canadians have a Camel (Camel 2F.1 *N8156*) at the Canadian Aviation and Space Museum. That aircraft came, via the Royal Air Force, to the Royal Canadian Air Force in 1924. The Canadian plane last flew in 1967. Another Sopwith Camel (Camel *B6291*) is restored and flying in California as part of the Javier Arango Collection. Camel F.1 *F6314* is on display at the Royal Air Force Museum, and the National Naval Aviation Museum in Florida has Camel F.1 *C8228*. Another (Camel *N6254*) was displayed in an Arkansas museum until it closed in 2010, whereupon the aircraft was sold to a museum in New Zealand to pay off debts.

Over the years there have been a number of reproductions of the Sopwith Camel built across the world. Numbers could be as high as 13 or 14, including those completed and those under construction.

The two Camels featured here both fly in New Zealand. One is the original Camel *N6254*, and the other is an authentic build by TVAL. Side by side, they are identical in all respects, other than the paint livery. Most people (unless they knew otherwise) would be unable to pick the original from the reproduction. That is how good the restoration and the reproduction are.

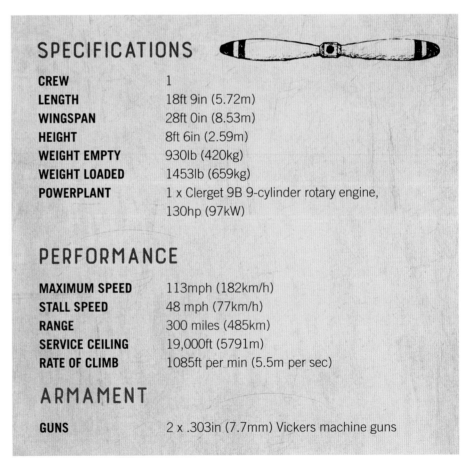

SPECIFICATIONS

CREW	1
LENGTH	18ft 9in (5.72m)
WINGSPAN	28ft 0in (8.53m)
HEIGHT	8ft 6in (2.59m)
WEIGHT EMPTY	930lb (420kg)
WEIGHT LOADED	1453lb (659kg)
POWERPLANT	1 x Clerget 9B 9-cylinder rotary engine, 130hp (97kW)

PERFORMANCE

MAXIMUM SPEED	113mph (182km/h)
STALL SPEED	48 mph (77km/h)
RANGE	300 miles (485km)
SERVICE CEILING	19,000ft (5791m)
RATE OF CLIMB	1085ft per min (5.5m per sec)

ARMAMENT

GUNS	2 x .303in (7.7mm) Vickers machine guns

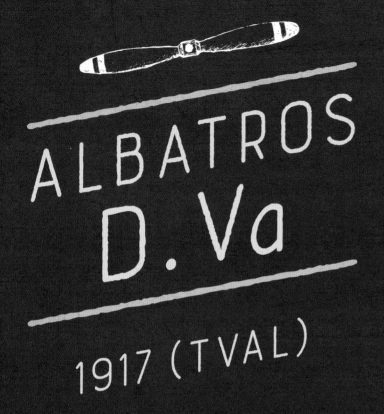

ALBATROS D.Va

1917 (TVAL)

Along with the Sopwith Camel and the Fokker Dr.1 Triplane, the Albatros is, without a doubt, one of my favourites of the Great War fighter collection. The first Albatros was the D.I, quickly followed by the D.II in late 1916. Following a pattern of continual improvement, the D.III arrived in early 1917. This, in turn, was followed by the D.IV, the D.V and the D.Va in mid-1917. The D.IIIs were an improved version of the previous model, and were characterised by a better rate of climb. They had twin-mounted machine guns that fired between the propeller blades, and the fuselage was plywood. This model achieved fame or notoriety (depending on what side you were on) with Jasta (Squadron) 11, under the leadership of Manfred von Richthofen (the Red Baron). He and his group of pilots shot down more enemy aircraft with the Albatros than they did with the Fokker Triplanes.

One of the weaknesses of the D.III Albatros was the upper wing structure and struts, with on more than one occasion pilots experiencing catastrophic wing failure. Most times, the pilots did not survive such an event. The D.Va finally addressed these problems by introducing heavier spars and steel-tube braces between the wings.

Over 4600 'D' series Albatros were built, with only two known original aircraft believed to have survived. They are both D.Va's. One is housed in the National Air and Space Museum in Washington, and the other is at the Australian War Memorial in Canberra.

When The Vintage Aviator Ltd decided to build a D.Va Albatros, they realised very early in the piece that they were in for a tough time, simply because of a lack of historical information on the aircraft. Some replicas had been built in the past, but unfortunately they were replicas in the truest sense of the word. They looked like an Albatros, but they were not accurate reproductions. The plans for these were readily available, so, armed with these as a starting point, TVAL took the step of going to Australia and, over several trips, using computer-guided laser technology were able to measure very accurately every inch of the original D.Va in the Canberra museum and reverse-engineer the plans. Combined with all of the other information they had collected, they were able to come up with what they believe to be a very accurate set of building plans for the original D.Va. The amount of research and measuring was simply mind-boggling, and they hadn't even started the build. The build was equally complicated, and, for those of you with a technical bent, the story of the build is detailed on the TVAL website. It is incredibly interesting, but far too detailed to reproduce in this book.

TVAL found an original D.IIIa Mercedes 6-cylinder engine, and completely stripped it down and rebuilt it, detailing every component for future builds as they went. Many of the engine accessory bits and pieces were manufactured in-house.

The prototype was completed in 2009, and a second was built for a client in Florida. In New Zealand, The Vintage Aviator Trust now has two of these reproduction originals, both D.Va's and both airworthy. They are painted in the liveries of actual pilots who flew these planes in the Great War.

The Albatros is a stunning-looking aircraft, and is just magic to watch in flight.

SPECIFICATIONS

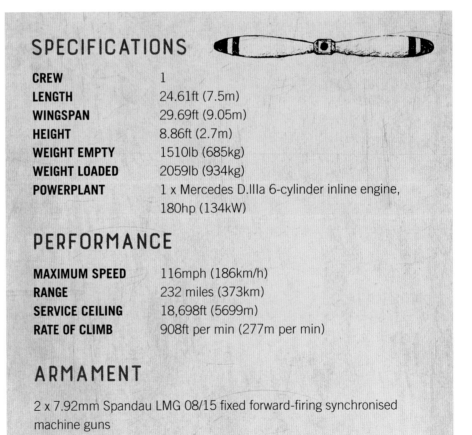

CREW	1
LENGTH	24.61ft (7.5m)
WINGSPAN	29.69ft (9.05m)
HEIGHT	8.86ft (2.7m)
WEIGHT EMPTY	1510lb (685kg)
WEIGHT LOADED	2059lb (934kg)
POWERPLANT	1 x Mercedes D.IIIa 6-cylinder inline engine, 180hp (134kW)

PERFORMANCE

MAXIMUM SPEED	116mph (186km/h)
RANGE	232 miles (373km)
SERVICE CEILING	18,698ft (5699m)
RATE OF CLIMB	908ft per min (277m per min)

ARMAMENT

2 x 7.92mm Spandau LMG 08/15 fixed forward-firing synchronised machine guns

August, one given to Werner Voss and the other to be shared by Manfred von Richthofen and his Jasta 11 Commander, Kurt Wolff. Voss had *103/17*, and Richthofen and Wolff shared *102/17*.

On 30 August, Voss shot down an Allied aircraft on his first flight. Richthofen did the same on his first flight, claiming his sixtieth kill. In just 24 days, Voss claimed 20 kills in the new Triplane.

With Richthofen and Voss visiting the Fokker factory, Kurt Wolff, recently returned from injury leave, took the Triplane *102/17* into battle against six top Allied fighters, with just his wingman in support in an Albatros. The wingman ended up fighting one of the planes, while Wolff ended up mixing it with the other five. The wingman, who survived the encounter, said that Wolff was flying brilliantly and seemed to have the upper hand. One of the

British pilots said that the Fokker Triplane was all over them and very difficult to get in one's sights. It was like there were five Triplanes. However, from official reports it seemed as though Wolff was overwhelmed and shot down. A photograph of his crashed Fokker shows her relatively whole, with her nose slightly into the ground and the three wings impacted forward over the nose, but still basically all there. It gives the impression that Wolff tried to fly the aircraft down and got pretty low before dying and crashing. (Wolff shot down 33 Allied aircraft.)

Exactly one week later, around the same time of day, Voss attacked six Allied aircraft, managing to put bullets into all six in another display of brilliant airmanship. Like Wolff a week earlier, it appeared that he, too, was overwhelmed by sheer numbers, and plummeted to earth with a solid impact that totally destroyed the aircraft. (Voss shot down 48 aircraft.) Manfred von Richthofen was shaken by the loss of the two men, whom he considered very good friends.

As the new planes came on-stream, several instances of top-wing failure occurred, with some more deaths, and some rather miraculous landings, including that of Manfred's brother, Lothar, whose wing broke up while in combat. He was seriously injured in the following crash-landing.

With these defects fixed, the highly manoeuvrable Triplane went on to write herself into the history books.

There are no surviving original Fokker Dr.1 Triplanes aircraft in the world, the last being destroyed in a museum during an Allied bombing raid in World War II. However, a number of replicas and reproductions have been built. Because of the scarcity of original engines, many have been powered with a Warner Scarab or Continental R-670 radial engine. A few have received vintage Le Rhône 9J or reproduction Oberursel Ur.II rotary engines.

In New Zealand, we are incredibly lucky to have eight replica/reproduction Fokker Dr.1 Triplanes, with seven of them registered to The Vintage Aviator Ltd. In 2015, at the Omaka Airshow at Blenheim, all eight of these Fokker Triplanes were seen flying in formation, a sight that has not been witnessed since the Great War. The seven Triplanes registered to The Vintage Aviator Ltd have all been painted up in the colours of Jasta 11 pilots of 1918. The seven aircraft are:

- *ZK-FOK* — is powered by a 220hp Continental radial engine, and was built by New Zealanders, the late Stuart Tantrum and John Lanham. The plane is painted to represent Manfred von Richthofen's aircraft.
- *ZK-FOC* — is powered by a 165hp 7-cylinder Warner Scarab radial engine, and was built in the United States, and painted in Leutnant Hans Weiss's colours.
- *ZK-JOC* — is also powered by a 165hp 7-cylinder Warner Scarab radial engine, and was built in the United States, and painted in Leutnant Werner Steinhäuser's colours.
- *ZK-JOB* — is powered by a 165hp 7-cylinder Warner Scarab radial engine, and was built in the United States, and painted in Leutnant Eberhardt Mohnicke's colours.
- *ZK-FOT* — is powered by a 165hp 7-cylinder Warner Scarab radial engine, and was built in the United States, and painted in Oberleutnant Lothar von Richthofen's colours.
- *ZK-JOK* — is powered by a 165hp 7-cylinder Warner Scarab radial engine, and was built in the United States, and painted in Jasta 11 aircraft original colours, unknown pilot.
- *ZK-JOG* — is powered by a 165hp 7-cylinder Warner Scarab radial engine, and was built in the United States, and painted in Leutnant Richard Wenzl's colours.

Of the pilots:
- Rittmeister Baron Manfred von Richthofen (Pour le Mérite) died on 21 April 1918, killed in action; 80 Allied aircraft shot down.
- Leutnant Hans Weiss died on 2 May 1918, killed in action; 16 Allied aircraft shot down.
- Leutnant Werner Steinhäuser died on 26 June 1918, killed in action; 10 kills.
- Leutnant Eberhardt Mohnicke was wounded in action September 1918, survived the war; eight kills.
- Oberleutnant Lothar von Richthofen (Pour le Mérite) was wounded in action, and died in 1922 as a pilot in a commercial airline accident; 40 kills.
- Leutnant Richard Wenzl transferred to Jasta 6, and survived the war; 12 Allied aircraft shot down.

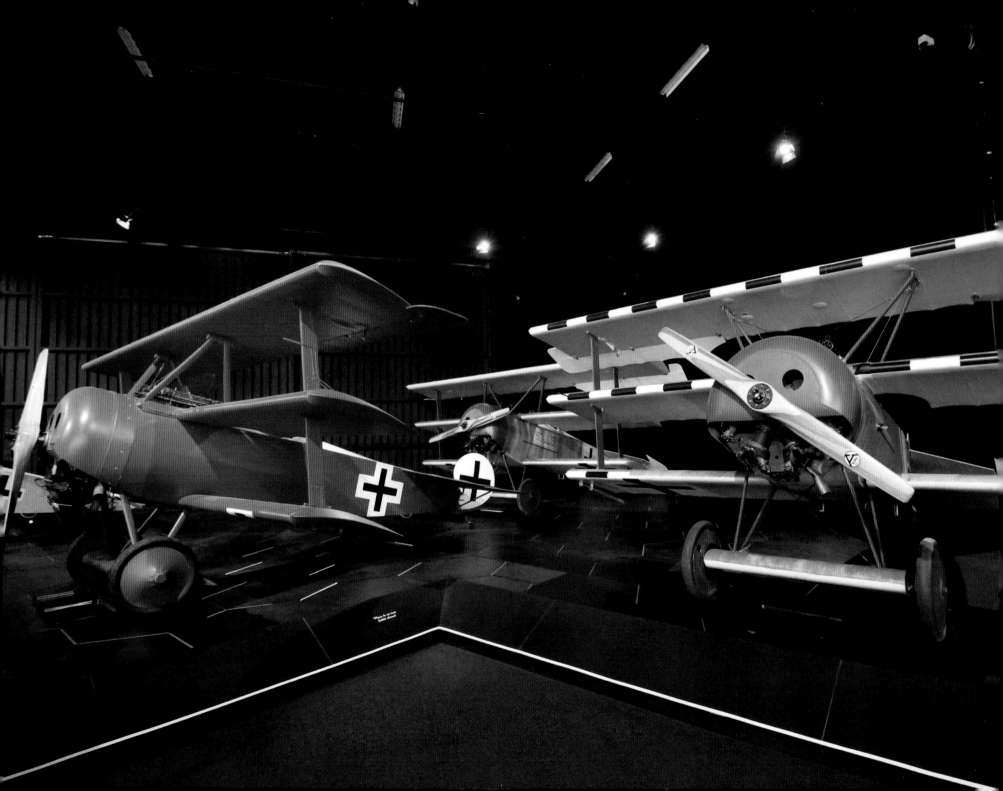

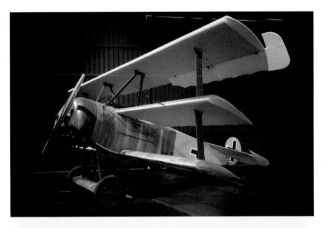

SPECIFICATIONS

CREW	1
LENGTH	18ft 11in (5.77m)
WINGSPAN	23ft 7in (7.19m)
HEIGHT	9ft 8in (2.95m)
WEIGHT EMPTY	895lb (406kg)
WEIGHT LOADED	1291lb (586kg)
POWERPLANT	1 x Oberursel Ur.II 9-cylinder rotary engine, 110hp (82kW)

PERFORMANCE

MAXIMUM SPEED	115mph (185km/h)
RANGE	185 miles (300km)
SERVICE CEILING	20,000ft (6100m)
RATE OF CLIMB	1130ft per min (5.7m per sec)

ARMAMENT

2 x 7.92mm (.312In) Spandau IMG 08 machine guns

FOKKER D.VII

1918 (TVAL)

In 1918, the Germans brought out the Fokker D.VII Biplane, a replacement for the famous Fokker Dr.1 Triplane. It was widely believed to be the best German fighter plane of the Great War. Arriving late in the war, the D.VII had a short career, but pilots praised the biplane's handling and ease of operation. Both the German Air Service and the German Navy took the D.VII into service, with over 1000 of them being manufactured and deployed. The D.VII proved to be fast, nimble and strong, and the agile fighter appeared to be able to best the British Sopwith Snipe in aerial combat. Production models were built by the Fokker and Albatros factories, with Albatros producing more than Fokker and at a better quality.

The powerplants installed numbered three. Initially, they were powered by the Mercedes 170hp–180hp D.IIIa engine. Later models had the Mercedes 180hp–200hp Mercedes D.IIIaü engine. By mid-1918, some were receiving the 'over-compressed' BMW IIIa engine. Developing 185hp, this straight six had higher compression and an altitude-adjusting carburettor, producing a marked increase in speed and climb rate at high altitude.

After the Armistice, the Allies confiscated large numbers of the Fokker D.VII for evaluation, with America, France, Great Britain and Canada receiving them as war prizes. The Polish, Hungarian, Dutch, Swiss and Belgian air forces also used them. In fact, the aircraft was so popular that Anthony Fokker smuggled the plans into the Netherlands and continued to manufacture them.

There appears to have been a few replica D.VIIs built over the years, the most notable being the aircraft built for the famous 1966 movie *The Blue Max*.

In New Zealand, we have a replica Fokker D.VII, which is, in fact, one of the replicas that were built for *The Blue Max*, and she has starred in other films since then. When she was placed in the care of The Vintage Aviator Ltd, they were surprised by her very average performance. She could not even hold a candle to the Sopwith Camel or the SE5a. Given that she had passed through many owners and was powered by a modern aircooled engine, a Gipsy Queen, it would not be unreasonable to expect the same performance recorded in history books, but even so it seemed to the TVAL pilots that she just felt heavy in the air and that the tail plane felt all wrong. A facelift was decided on, and when stripped it was found that the construction was certainly not authentic, and a lot of weight had been added by using easily acquired materials that were a lot heavier than the original specifications. The exercise became a bit more than a refresh, with the added plan to reduce the weight and, where possible, get as close to authentic as possible with the replica. The story of her rebuild on the TVAL website is as interesting as it is detailed, and for the technically inclined is well worth a read. Today, this beautiful replica would fool most of us, as she really does look the part and is great to see flying our skies.

SPECIFICATIONS

CREW	1
LENGTH	22ft 10in (6.95m)
WINGSPAN	29ft 2in (8.96m)
HEIGHT	9ft 0in (2.75m)
WEIGHT EMPTY	1477lb (670kg)
WEIGHT LOADED	1995lb (905kg)
POWERPLANT	1 x Mercedes D.IIIa or D.IIIaü or BMW IIIa 6-cylinder inline liquid-cooled engine, 170hp–200hp range (126kW–149kW)

PERFORMANCE

MAXIMUM SPEED	117mph (189km/h)
ENDURANCE	90 min
SERVICE CEILING	17,999ft (5486m)
RATE OF CLIMB	772ft per min (235m per min) with Mercedes engine; 1874ft per min (9.52m per sec) with BMW engine

ARMAMENT

2 x 7.92 Spandau LMG 08/15 synchronised machine guns

SOPWITH SNIPE

1918 (TVAL)

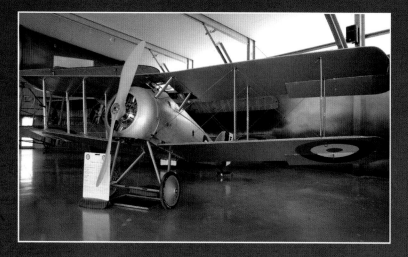

Before I started this book, I was aware of a number of World War I fighter aircraft, although the only ones I had seen in photographs and duly recognised were the Albatros, the Fokker Triplane and the Sopwith Camel. I had heard of the Sopwith 'Pup', the Sopwith 'Tripe', the 'Fee' and the Nieuport, but had no idea of what they looked like. In the movies, I had seen that at the time the aircraft were biplanes, but I was so immersed in the stories that I really didn't study the planes that much. So some of the very early aircraft have been real eye-openers. The later 1918 versions, for example, I was not really aware of. The Fokkers that followed the Fokker Triplane were new to me, as was the Sopwith Snipe.

By following these aircraft through the Great War sequence, I should not have been surprised about these later arrivals, as it seems the British and the Germans were playing leapfrog in an effort to gain air superiority. The Snipe was Britain's attempt to do just that. Following on from the successful 'Pup', 'Tripehound' and 'Camel', the Snipe gave the Brits another edge for a few weeks. Arriving at the Front in late 1918, the Snipe remained in production until September 1919, with examples flying in the air force until 1926.

The Snipe was a nice plane to fly, and fortunately had lost most of the vices of the Camel. They were highly manoeuvrable, although by 1918 standards they were not very fast. They were great at high altitudes and had an awesome rate of climb, which more than compensated for the perceived lack of speed. They were powered by a Bentley BR2 rotary engine (the last rotary engine to be used by the air force). Their armament was the same as the Sopwith Camel, and they had a top speed of 121mph. Just under 500 were produced, and there was just the one variant.

There are two original Snipes, both in museums: one at the National Air and Space Museum in Washington, and the other at the Canada Aviation and Space Museum at Rockcliffe, just outside Ottawa. Reproductions are few and far between, with one very detailed version being built by Antique Aero in California. The Vintage Aviator built an airworthy Snipe, complete with an original Bentley engine, that was sold to Kermit Weeks for his Fantasy of Flight Museum in Florida. They also built a static version for the Royal Air Force Museum in Britain. According to the civil aviation register, in 2015 there are two airworthy Snipes registered to The Vintage Aviator Ltd and flying in New Zealand, although one is believed to have been shipped to England in mid-2015. These Snipes are another superb reproduction aircraft that reek of authenticity, with an amazing quality build.

SPECIFICATIONS

CREW	1
LENGTH	19ft 10in (6.05m)
WINGSPAN	31ft 1in (9.48m)
HEIGHT	9ft 6in (2.90m)
WEIGHT EMPTY	1312lb (596kg)
WEIGHT LOADED	2020lb (918kg)
POWERPLANT	1 x Bentley BR2 rotary engine, 230hp (172kW)

PERFORMANCE

MAXIMUM SPEED	121mph (195km/h)
ENDURANCE	3 hr
SERVICE CEILING	19,500ft (5945m)
RATE OF CLIMB	5 min 10 sec to 6600ft (1980m)
	18 min 50 sec to 15,000ft (4570m)

ARMAMENT

GUNS	2 x .303in (7.7mm) Vickers machine guns
BOMBS	4 x 25lb (11kg) bombs

FOKKER D.VIII (TVAL)

1918

The Fokker D.VIII is a monoplane (one-winged), and was first seen on the Western Front in August 1918. However, they were quickly withdrawn because of 'structural weaknesses', before being reinstated in October 1918. Only 85 went in to service by the time the war ended in November 1918, but in the three weeks they saw service they proved to be a satisfactory fighter. They were sent to Jasta 11, the most famous fighter wing of Geschwader 1 (von Richthofen's outfit). The Fokker D.VIII has the honour of scoring the last aerial victory of the Great War.

The Allied airmen nicknamed her the 'Flying Razor', because of her shape and parasol wing design. The parasol wing design allowed for the wing to be suspended above the fuselage by way of support struts. If you imagine a typical biplane, and then remove the lower wing structure, you will get the picture. Armament was what was by now the accepted forward-mounted Spandau machine gun synchronised to fire through the propeller. The engine was an Oberursel Ur.II rotary engine of 110hp.

The only known original survivor is preserved at the Gianni Caproni Museum of Aeronautics in Trento, Italy.

The featured Fokker D.VIII is a factory-built original authentic reproduction, built by The Vintage Aviator Ltd. Even the engine is a TVAL-built Oberursel, manufactured to original specifications. I was fortunate to see this beautiful little fighter flying at an open day at Hood Aerodrome in Masterton. It is a delight to see her in the air. She looks quite fragile in comparison to the Albatros or the SE5a, but that really is quite misleading, as they proved to be quite a robust and effective fighter in their short career.

The workmanship on this aircraft, like anything TVAL touch, is absolutely stunning. Almost unbelievable is the incredible re-creation by TVAL of the Oberursel rotary engine: it is totally correct to the original specifications. What an achievement!

SPECIFICATIONS

CREW	1
LENGTH	19ft 3in (5.86m)
WINGSPAN	27ft 4in (8.34m)
HEIGHT	8ft 6in (2.6m)
WEIGHT EMPTY	893lb (405kg)
WEIGHT LOADED	1334lb (605kg)
POWERPLANT	1 x Oberursel Ur.II 9-cylinder aircooled rotary engine, 110hp (82 kW)

PERFORMANCE

MAXIMUM SPEED	127mph (204km/h)
ENDURANCE	1.5 hr
SERVICE CEILING	19,685ft (6000m)
RATE OF CLIMB	1640ft per min (8.333m per sec)

ARMAMENT

2 x .312in (7.92mm) Spandau MG08 machine guns

AIRCRAFT OF THE 1920S AND 1930S

In this section of the book I have endeavoured to capture mostly civil aircraft that were designed or built in the late 1920s and the 1930s. A number of the aircraft featured ended up being used by the Allies in World War II, some for clandestine flights, others as trainers. However, as most were not primarily built for military use, or were built as initial military trainers, they have been featured in this section. Some of the aircraft are re-creations of the original, most are originals. Many had long production lives, some going on post-war. Although some featured aircraft were built post-war, they were in fact 1930s designs, and the exact same models were in production pre-war. Many had long post-war histories in civil aviation.

Many of these aircraft retained fabric-covered fuselages and wings, but it was through this period that we saw the change to plywood fuselages and to fully aluminium bodies, fuselage and wings. It was also the period of change from biplanes to mono-winged aircraft. With the advent of the Douglas Dakota DC3, we saw the coming of the modern age of airliners, both in shape and in design. Without a doubt, the DC3 was a turning point in civil aircraft design and heralded a new age in aviation.

The Waco was one of the first planes to use hydraulic suspension on the landing gear, and Marty has fitted disc brakes, featuring 6-piston callipers. These are discreetly hidden under the very attractive and functional wheel spats.

The first Waco Taperwing flew in 1928; Marty's Waco is a 1992-built reproduction. Marty first saw this Waco at the Oshkosh airshow in Wisconsin some years back. He was greatly taken with her, and wanted to buy one. His wife said, 'Don't be ridiculous.' A Mustang three-quarter-scale kitset later, Marty saw this very Waco Taperwing for sale on the Barnstormers website. He shot off an enquiry about her, but the owner had second thoughts and withdrew her from sale. Disappointed, Marty turned his attention elsewhere and bought a Boeing Stearman (see the story on page 111). Some three years later, Marty received a mysterious email from the States, saying 'Marty ring me' along with a telephone number. Somewhat mystified but definitely curious, Marty rang the number, and to his surprise it was the elderly gentleman who owned the Waco. He said he wasn't very good at writing, hence the very short email. He also said that Marty's original enquiry had been the first of many, so he was giving Marty first option, as he wanted to sell the Waco. A week later, Marty was on his way to Chicago to arrange shipping home his new toy.

The engine in the Waco is a Jacobs, and is one of the few aero engines that runs a single magneto and a single distributor. (Most aero engines run twin magnetos.) You start the engine on the distributor, and the engine shakes and vibrates like crazy until you switch it to the magneto, whereupon it stops shaking and settles down to a smooth-running engine. Because of this feature, the motors have earned the nickname 'Shaky Jake'. The Waco's powerplant develops 275hp (the same horsepower as my 1956 classic Packard car) and cruises at a maximum speed of 150mph (twice the cruising speed of my Packard). Marty has undertaken a full rebuild of the Waco, and has learned a huge amount about her on the restoration journey. The end result is just stunning and an absolute credit to Marty.

We were able to catch Marty and the Waco in flight in early 2016.

SPECIFICATIONS

CREW	1
PASSENGERS	1
LENGTH	22ft 6in (6.86m)
WINGSPAN	30ft 3in (9.3m)
HEIGHT	9ft (2.74m)
WEIGHT EMPTY	1900lb (861kg)
POWERPLANT	1 x Jacobs R-775-B2 engine, 275hp (205kW)

PERFORMANCE

MAXIMUM SPEED	150mph (241km/h)
RANGE	650 miles (965.6km)
SERVICE CEILING	10,000ft (3048m)
RATE OF CLIMB	Enough! (according to Marty)

DE HAVILLAND
DH GIPSY
MOTH

1929

On the journey of writing this book, I have come across some neat stories. This is one of them. The predecessor to the Tiger Moth was the Gipsy Moth. First appearing in 1928, this particular featured aircraft, designated a DH60GII, is a 1929 model. She is owned by Jan and Jerry Chisum, both well-known pilots in the Tiger Moth Club in New Zealand. Jerry first flew a Tiger Moth in 1972, with Jan doing the same some 13 years later. So folks, plenty of experience here. But that is only part of the story. The Gipsy Moth that they own was once owned by Jan's father. He purchased the aircraft in 1934, after she had already flown from England to North Africa, to the Middle East and also through Burma to Bangkok (at that time called Siam). Jan's dad flew *G-AAJO* (or 'Jo', as he called her) from England to Sydney. He had her shipped to Auckland, then flew her the last part of the journey back home to Hawke's Bay.

When war broke out in 1939, the government seized the Gipsy Moth and intended using her as a trainer. However, the new Tiger Moths were much better suited to the task, partly due to their cockpit's accessibility, and the little Gipsy languished through the war with very little use. Afterwards she passed through several hands, including syndicates, flying through to the mid-1960s. Eventually, she was laid up and became dilapidated, to the extent of not being airworthy. In the early 1980s, she was bought by Lee Middleton from the Pukekohe area, with the intention of restoring her back to airworthiness. So began a near 30-year restoration.

The Gipsy Moth is a DH60GII model, which means she has a wooden-framed fuselage and engine mounts. *ADT* (Alfa, Delta, Tango) is still powered by her original Gipsy engine as first delivered. The later Gipsy Moths, designated 'GIII', had a steel-framed fuselage and an inverted engine, which became known as the 'Gipsy Major engine'.

Jan always kept track of the restoration and, with Jerry, visited Lee when the rebuild was complete. A couple of years later, Lee allowed Jan to fly 'Jo' to Bridge Pa to commemorate the little aircraft's arrival exactly 75 years earlier.

The owner maintained that he would keep the aircraft forever, but Jan and Jerry continued to keep in touch, and several years down the track Lee got interested in sail planes (gliders) and decided to sell the Gipsy Moth. That was in 2012, so 78 years after her dad first bought the Gipsy, 'Jo' was back in the family. Jan was able to fly her home, and the aircraft has remained very active ever since.

Just recently the aircraft starred in the making of a TV movie of the life of Jean Batten. The engine was being rebuilt at the time, so Colin Smith of the Croydon Aircraft Company kindly lent them another motor for the movie. The Moth was coated in silver to be the same as the Gypsy Moth in which Jean Batten made her record-breaking England-to-Australia flight. Later, Jean turned around and flew back to England! If you ever get to see the movie, you'll see that the aircraft is piloted by Jan.

As we were writing this, Jan described the plane as being dressed in drag, and she and Jerry posed for the photograph shown here of her in 'drag'. The other photographs are of the aircraft in her normal colours, and have kindly been supplied by Jan and Jerry. The Gipsy with her rebuilt engine and original colour scheme will be back in the air by the time this book is on the shelves. The black-and-white photographs show the aircraft in 1934 when she belonged to Jan's dad, and that is him in the cockpit.

Both Jan and Jerry say the aircraft is beautiful to fly. In their own words: 'She's a sweet little aircraft.' What a great story!

SPECIFICATIONS

CREW	2 (pilot and passenger)
LENGTH	23ft 11in (7.29m)
WINGSPAN	30ft 0in (9.14m)
HEIGHT	8ft 9.5in (2.68m)
WEIGHT EMPTY	930lb (421kg)
WEIGHT LOADED	1750lb (793kg)
POWERPLANT	1 x de Havilland Gipsy II, 4-cylinder, upright inline piston engine, 120hp (90kW)

PERFORMANCE

MAXIMUM SPEED	105mph (170km/h)
CRUISE SPEED	85mph (137km/h)
RANGE	400 miles (565km)
SERVICE CEILING	14,500ft (4420m)
RATE OF CLIMB	700ft per min (2.5m per sec)

DE HAVILLAND DH82a TIGER MOTH

1931

Down Under, these aircraft are a bit of a legend. Designed in the 1930s, they were used extensively as a trainer aircraft, both for private pilots and of course in the Royal Air Force (RAF), and here in New Zealand in the Royal New Zealand Air Force. In fact, nearly all New Zealand wartime pilots received their initial training in the Tiger Moth. After the war, many of the Tiger Moths were used in civil operation, both commercially and as recreational aircraft.

The Tiger was derived from the Gipsy Moth, with the main criteria being a wider front cockpit that would allow its occupant to exit easily while wearing a parachute. Other improvements were incorporated at the same time. From the outset the Tiger Moth proved to be reliable, easy to maintain and cheap to run. They also proved to be a great trainer. They entered service with the RAF in 1932, and were their primary trainer until 1952. They are fully aerobatic, but apparently require a firm hand when doing aerobatics.

In New Zealand, after the war, a number were used for aerial topdressing (cropdusting) before being replaced by the Fletchers and Air Trucks in the 1950s. Many of these Tiger Moths passed into private hands at that point, and, according to the Civil Aviation Authority register, there are still some 34 Tiger Moths flying in New Zealand, which is a great number, considering estimates put airworthy models across the world at about 250, and static models at about 40, which includes a few in New Zealand.

During the sojourn of writing this book, I have seen examples around the country, with four flying into Whitianga, others at Ardmore, and three beautiful examples flying at Wanaka. I always have enjoyed watching Tiger Moths in flight, and seem to have witnessed them quite often during the years of my life. Often, sitting on the deck at our beach house in Whitianga, I watch our local resident Tiger Moth lazily going through her aerobatic routine. I never tire of watching her. I do not know whether I have been in the right place at the right time to see these endearing old planes in flight, or whether we just have so many still flying that one can't help running into them. Whatever, I hope I continue to see these legendary aircraft in the air.

SPECIFICATIONS

CREW	2 (instructor and student)
LENGTH	23ft 11in (7.34m)
WINGSPAN	29ft 4in (8.94m)
HEIGHT	8ft 9in (2.68m)
WEIGHT EMPTY	1115lb (506kg)
WEIGHT LOADED	1825lb (828kg)
POWERPLANT	1 x Gipsy Major engine, 130hp (97kW)

PERFORMANCE

MAXIMUM SPEED	109mph (175km/h)
CRUISE SPEED	67mph (119km/h)
RANGE	302 miles (486km)
SERVICE CEILING	13,600ft (4145m)
RATE OF CLIMB	673ft per min (205m per min)

DE HAVILLAND DH83C FOX MOTH

1932

During the war she served with the Royal New Zealand Air Force from 1943 to 1948, before passing into the hands of NAC (National Airways Corporation). Subsequently, she passed through several further owners' hands and was based in the United States from 1974 to 1984, before moving on to England. She returned to New Zealand, and was restored to her original livery and call sign in 1997. She is a significant aircraft, as she was the first aircraft registered in New Zealand to carry passengers commercially. She is owned by the Croydon Aviation Heritage Centre.

Next door at the Croydon Aviation Company, Colin and Maeva Smith and their staff have just completed a total restoration of a third Fox Moth, which at the time of our interview had already been test-flown. The aircraft looks absolutely great and will make a great addition to our airworthy heritage aircraft. At the time of writing, the Fox Moth was complete other than finishing and fitting her wheel spats.

Thinking about the Fox Moth being New Zealand's first commercial airliner makes you realise that from such small beginnings, look at where we have got to now.

Both of the Fox Moths I have witnessed flying look beautiful in the air and are a wonderful reminder of the 1930s–1940s era.

SPECIFICATIONS

CREW	1
PASSENGERS	3
LENGTH	25ft 9in (7.85m)
WINGSPAN	30ft 11in (9.43m)
HEIGHT	8ft 9in (2.62m)
WEIGHT EMPTY	1071lb (487kg)
WEIGHT LOADED	2000lb (909kg)
POWERPLANT	1 x de Havilland Gipsy Major engine, 130hp (97kW)

PERFORMANCE

MAXIMUM SPEED	106mph (171km/h)
CRUISE SPEED	91mph (147km/h)
RANGE	425 miles (684km)
SERVICE CEILING	12,700ft (3870m)
RATE OF CLIMB	450ft per min (2.3m per sec)

STAMPE SV4A

1933

The Stampe SV4A was designed by Jean Stampe in 1932/1933, with their first flight in 1933. Jean, a former test pilot and personal pilot to the King of Belgium, was the agent for the DH60 Moth, the predecessor of the Tiger Moth. He wanted to improve the design and make the Stampe highly aerobatic. He, along with his partner Vertongen, designed them primarily for military use. Only 35 Stampes were built before the war. With an invasion by Hitler imminent, Stampe put his designs and planes in hiding for the duration of the war. After the war, production began again in Belgium and, under licence, in France and Algeria. The Stampe's main use was as a trainer in the various air forces. Production went through to 1955. Altogether another 35 aircraft were made by Stampe, along with another combined total of 940 aircraft built in France and Algeria.

The Stampe has enjoyed fame in a number of movies, starring both as a German and a British aircraft. They played as German aircraft in *The Blue Max* and *Von Richthofen and Brown*, they were made to look like SE5a's (British) in *Aces High*, and they played as the Belgian Stampe in *Indiana Jones and the Last Crusade*. The other well-known film they featured in was *High Road to China*, again as an SE5a look-alike.

The featured Stampe SV4A has a production date of 1946. Her owner and pilot is Lars Fellman. This particular aircraft, a fully aerobatic model, belonged to a flying school in France in the 1960s. Lars purchased her from the girlfriend/partner of the owner, who had been killed in a light aircraft accident in the Alps. The previous owner had been a naval captain and a medical doctor, and went by the name of Xavier Maniquet. If that name sounds familiar to New Zealanders, it's because Xavier was one of the French agents involved in the *Rainbow Warrior* bombing incident.

Lars received the Stampe in a 20-foot container, and reassembled the aircraft in his hanger on his lifestyle block at South Head. His first New Zealand test-flight was on 9 May 2011.

He initially flew her on her French registration until that expired, whereupon she was given New Zealand registration.

The Stampe SV4A has a three-tone paint livery, with the main colour being white. There is some black on the fuselage, and the wings and tail feature a stunning pattern of red stripes like the rising sun. She just looks so attractive.

So what about our owner/pilot? One of the best parts of writing books is the people you meet. Lars is a most interesting person who has lived a most interesting life. He was born in Finland by the coast, and was brought up with a love of the sea and yachts. He has competed in two Around-the-World Whitbread races on Finnish entries, and met and fell for a Kiwi girl on a race layover in Auckland. Lars gained his pilot's licence in 1968 and got into aerobatics soon after. He was lucky to be mentored by Finland's top aerobatic pilot, and moved into aerobatic competition and worked as an instructor in aerobatics. At some point in time, Lars decided he needed a real career and went to work for Carlsberg Beer, over the years managing plants in Denmark, Sweden, Italy, England and Germany. While in Denmark he decided to build a helicopter. When he transferred to Sweden, he took the helicopter with him, completing it there. The helicopter then followed him around the world, and now resides in his hangar here in New Zealand. Since arriving here in 2006, Lars has built a kitset Savage fixed-wing aeroplane, assembled the Stampe, and has just completed a second kitset Bearhawk aircraft. He is 72 years young, and still flies regularly. He even has his own airstrip on his lifestyle block, and believe me it is not for the faint-hearted. It runs down an incline, along a flat, then up another incline, and you can only take off and land in one direction. Fortunately, it faces into the prevailing wind. I asked Lars what it was like to take off on. His reply: 'A little tricky.' Then came the obvious question: 'What's it like to land on?' His reply: 'Oh, that's a little more tricky.'

I have to admit, our afternoon visit with Lars was highly enjoyable. He is a mine of information and such an interesting person. He maintains that he is a lousy engineer. (Yeah, right — another Tui's moment.) I am a coachbuilder by trade and have designed and built caravans, motorhomes and boats, so I know good work when I see it. The attention to detail in all of the planes Lars has built, along with the assembly and presentation of the Stampe, is absolutely excellent.

Back to the Stampe, there is absolutely no doubt that this is a very special aircraft and a very pretty bird. There are only two currently flying in New Zealand, so in this part of the world she is very rare.

It is with much sadness that we record that Lars Fellman passed away peacefully at his home a few weeks before this book went to print.

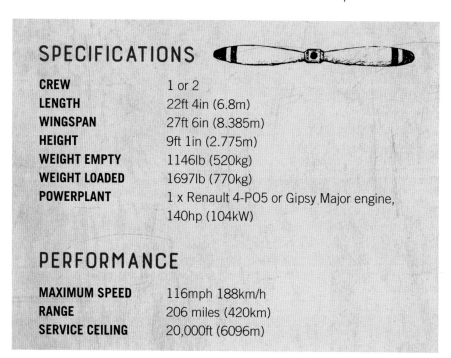

SPECIFICATIONS

CREW	1 or 2
LENGTH	22ft 4in (6.8m)
WINGSPAN	27ft 6in (8.385m)
HEIGHT	9ft 1in (2.775m)
WEIGHT EMPTY	1146lb (520kg)
WEIGHT LOADED	1697lb (770kg)
POWERPLANT	1 x Renault 4-PO5 or Gipsy Major engine, 140hp (104kW)

PERFORMANCE

MAXIMUM SPEED	116mph 188km/h
RANGE	206 miles (420km)
SERVICE CEILING	20,000ft (6096m)

DE HAVILLAND
DH89b
DOMINIE/RAPIDE

1934

Way back in December 1965, when I was a 15-year-old teenager, our family left Hamilton in our brand-new Triumph 2000, with our 1962 Liteweight Silver Planet caravan on the back, for our first big odyssey to the South Island. We shipped down to Christchurch, then toured the lower half of the Mainland. While at Queenstown, my dad decided that we should all take a tourist flight to Milford Sound. The plane we chartered was a De Havilland Rapide/Dominie. We were introduced to it as a Dominie, but until very recently I didn't realise the Dominie and the Rapide are exactly the same aircraft. Apparently, when the military impressed them into service, they gave them the name of Dominie. Goodness knows why. What was wrong with Rapide?

I have remembered that flight vividly for the past 50-plus years. It was a fine day, and flying across the Southern Alps was spectacular. We came in very steeply at Milford Sound; I remember that well, because the pressure build-up gave me earache. We flew out at low level along the Sounds, before climbing back over the Southern Alps, and landing back at Frankton Arm in Queenstown.

When I came face-to-face with a Dominie in Tauranga recently, I got very excited, explaining to my wife the aforementioned flight in one of these twin-engined, fabric-covered eight-passenger biplanes. We were able to climb inside and get some nice photographs. A few weeks later we caught some great photographs of her flying at the Classic Flyers show in Tauranga. Upon talking to the pilot, he told me that there are still two airworthy Rapides/Dominies flying in New Zealand, the other being at Mandeville, just out of Gore at the bottom of the South Island.

A few weeks later, we were heading down to the South Island for six weeks (in our vintage 1956 Liteweight Kiwi caravan) to gather in more aircraft for this book. In my planning for the trip, I rang Croydon Aircraft Company to make an appointment to see them. Telling them what I was about, and in conversation with co-owner Maeva, I mentioned my flight over the Alps, and how I would love to find the Rapide/Dominie that I flew in. Surprise, surprise! They have the exact same plane in their line-up. Yes, she is the old Queenstown plane, and she is the other airworthy Rapide/Dominie still flying. Now I am normally very cool, calm and collected, but I do have to admit I became very excited about this.

These aircraft were designed in 1933, with the prototype being produced in 1934. They became a very popular short-haul passenger plane, carrying one crew and eight passengers. By the outbreak of war, the military in Great Britain impressed many of them into service and ordered another 500 built, bringing the total build to 731. Post-war, many went into civilian roles, and by 1958 there were still 81 examples on the British register. We received some 14 Rapides/Dominies into the Royal New Zealand Air Force, and they were active from 1939 through to 1953, before being sold for civil use. They went on to fly for NAC (National Airways Corporation), Air Travel (NZ) Ltd, Mount Cook Airline and Cook Strait Airways Ltd.

Today, apparently only seven have survived, worldwide. One is static in a museum in Manchester, England, another the same in France, and one on display in a museum in Ohio. The remaining four are still airworthy, one based at Membury Airfield, Berkshire, England; another flies with the Military Aviation Museum in Virginia Beach, USA. And little old New Zealand has the other two.

The photographs show not only both Dominies/Rapides, but also a third one under restoration for an Australian customer. The restoration is proceeding slowly, as and when the customer's finances permit. By my reckoning, that will take the total number of survivors to eight!

It was an absolute thrill to see the South Island Rapide, and actually climb on board and sit once again in the very seat that I sat in as a 15-year-old lad,

more than half a century on. Her history was much as previously mentioned, with this particular aircraft flying for NAC from 1947 to 1961, when she was purchased by Ritchie Air Services of Te Anau and flown mainly into Fiordland and Milford Sound. Ritchie later merged with Mount Cook Airline in the 1960s, and she was then based in Queenstown doing trips to Milford Sound. This is where I first came across her in 1965. She was sold in 1978 and was fully restored, re-emerging in NAC colours. She has been owned by the Croydon Aviation Heritage Trust since 2006.

After seeing her, a week later, at the Warbirds Over Wanaka airshow, it was an even greater thrill to see her flying once more and to be able to capture her on camera, mid-flight.

SPECIFICATIONS

CREW	1
PASSENGERS	8
LENGTH	34ft 6in (10.5m)
WINGSPAN	48ft 0in (14.6m)
HEIGHT	10ft 3in (3.1m)
WEIGHT EMPTY	3230lb (1460kg)
WEIGHT LOADED	5500lb (2490kg)
POWERPLANT	2 x de Havilland Gipsy Six inline engines, 200hp (149kW) each

PERFORMANCE

MAXIMUM SPEED	157mph (253km/h)
RANGE	520 miles (837km)
SERVICE CEILING	16,700ft (5090m)
RATE OF CLIMB	867ft per min (4.3m per sec)

BOEING STEARMAN

1934

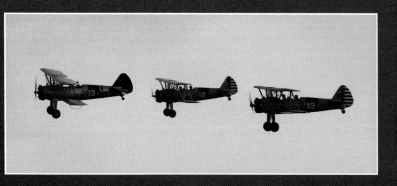

The Boeing Stearmans, as we see them here, were originally designed in 1934 as a military trainer for the US Army and Navy. The navy painted theirs yellow; the army, yellow and blue. The planes were fully aerobatic. The hallmark of the Stearmans was that they were all well-made and highly sophisticated for their time. Also, they were very expensive to buy. It was when Boeing took over the Stearman Company that they became known as the 'Boeing Stearman'.

After the war, having been superseded as military trainers, they started a second phase in their lives as cropdusters (topdressers), airshow aircraft, aerial photography aircraft, and as movie stars! When the famous Reno Air Races started, there was even a Boeing Stearman racing class. These days, they are sought after by vintage aviators as a 'classic aircraft', and either put into museums or restored and flown as recreational aircraft. There are several examples flying in New Zealand, with, I believe, three of them available for paying rides.

Of the four featured here that we have been fortunate enough to have captured with our camera lens, two are in private ownership and two are in syndicate ownership, with one of the syndicates attached to the Classic Flyers Museum in Tauranga. Two are painted yellow in the traditional US Navy colours, and the other two in US army colours, with one of them romantically called *Witchita Gal*. The army colours are a striking yellow and blue. All four planes are in immaculate condition and look just stunning. The two yellow ones are domiciled at Tauranga Aiport, along with a third Stearman (see the Classic Flyers Museum, Mount Maunganui, on page 284) at the same airport. The other featured Stearman is owned by a syndicate and is based at Ardmore in South Auckland.

Marty, the owner of one of the yellow Stearmans, who had shares in the Classic Flyers' Stearman, had decided that he would like to own one just for himself. He found a good one on the internet, and mentioned to his friend Mike that he was going stateside to buy the Stearman. Mike, also a private pilot, had some time earlier decided to build a three-quarter-scale kitset Mustang fighter replica, and had convinced Marty to build one as well. Having completed those together, Mike had no intention of missing out on Marty's next adventure, and decided to accompany him stateside. All was well with the Stearman purchase, and Marty and Mike had such fun flying her that Mike decided to buy a Stearman for himself … as you do. They had bought Marty's Stearman in Galesburg, Wisconsin. They found another example in Iowa, so flew down to inspect her. Another great find, and another great purchase. Together they flew the two Stearmans back to Galesburg. Having to wait another 10 days for a container to arrive, they spent the time flying around the Mississippi and Illinois areas, before stripping the planes down for shipment to New Zealand. Both Marty and Mike agree that it was a great time, with fantastic flying. They have owned the Stearmans for four years.

My wife, Marilyn, and I ran into the immaculate *Witchita Gal* yellow-and-blue Stearman quite by accident. We were at our beach house in Whitianga, and Marilyn was experimenting with a brilliant new telephoto lens she had bought for the camera. We decided to go down to the local airstrip and experiment with the lens, doing ground-to-air shots on any planes that happened to fly in. Sitting all alone at the airport was this stunning Stearman. We couldn't find the pilot, despite extensive enquiry. No one at the airport seemed to know who she belonged to. We photographed her as much as we could, then left a card with the owner of the Airport Café, who said that she would phone us if she found the pilot. We had just got home when the telephone rang, so we shot back down and met the pilot, Andrew Hope, and his partner. They were already in their flying suits, but Andrew was most accommodating. He is part-owner of the Stearman, a warbird pilot on other aircraft, and flies as a commercial pilot on airliners. We were able to get some great photographs of *Witchita Gal* along with our first ground-to-air shots.

SPECIFICATIONS

CREW	2
LENGTH	24ft 9in (7.54m)
WINGSPAN	32ft 2in (9.81m)
HEIGHT	9ft 8in (3m)
WING AREA	298sqft (27.7sqm)
WEIGHT EMPTY	1931lb (878kg)
WEIGHT MAX. TAKEOFF	2635lb (1200kg)
POWERPLANT	1x Continental R-670-5 7-cylinder aircooled radial engine, 220hp (164kW)

PERFORMANCE

MAXIMUM SPEED	135mph (217km/h)
CRUISE SPEED	96mph (155km/h)
SERVICE CEILING	13,200ft (4024m)
RATE OF CLIMB	10,000ft in 17.3 min (3048m in 17.3 min)

DE HAVILLAND DRAGONFLY

1935

The Dragonfly is not dissimilar in looks to the Dragon Rapide, but is smaller and has a higher aspect ratio and swept-back wings. They are substantially faster than the Rapide. In New Zealand, they were used commercially in the 1940s and 1950s, mainly on the West Coast of the South Island. Flying out of Croydon Airport, they built up to around seven in number.

The De Havilland Dragonfly presented here is one of just two airworthy examples in the world. The other is in a private collection in the United Kingdom. This Dragonfly was produced in 1936, just a year after the first one was built. It was first registered in England and used for executive transport. Only 67 Dragonflies were built. The fuselage is a monocoque shell of plywood with spruce stringers covered in fabric.

This particular aircraft, besides flying in New Zealand, has also flown in Australia and the United States. She was restored in England in 1986, returning to New Zealand in 1996. Since then she has been registered as *ZK-AYR* (Alfa, Yankee, Romeo), and became an early addition to the Croydon Aviation Heritage Trust Collection. In addition to giving standard flights, *ZK-AYR* has in the past been used as an air ambulance and for aerial photo-survey work.

What really appeals to me, with both the Dragonfly and the Rapide, is their stately elegance. They are both beautiful-looking aircraft and, if it is at all possible, a little Art Deco in their appearance. I just love them.

SPECIFICATIONS

CREW	1
PASSENGERS	3
LENGTH	31ft 8in (9.65m)
WINGSPAN	43ft 0in (13.11m)
HEIGHT	9ft 2in (2.79m)
WEIGHT EMPTY	2500lb (1134kg)
WEIGHT LOADED	4000lb (1814kg)
POWERPLANT	2 x Gipsy Major II engines, 142hp (106kW) each

PERFORMANCE

MAXIMUM SPEED	144mph (232km/h)
RANGE	625 miles (1000km)
SERVICE CEILING	18,000ft (5515m)
RATE OF CLIMB	875ft per min (4.5m per sec)

DOUGLAS DAKOTA DC3

1936

The DC3, as it is commonly called in New Zealand, is a legend in the world of aviation. Designed in the 1930s, they effectively revolutionised passenger air travel in the 1930s and 1940s. They were used extensively in World War II as transporters, and post-war were used by many domestic airlines worldwide. These factors probably make them one of the most significant aircraft ever made.

In civil form they were known as the 'DC3', and 697 were built. In military use, they were designated 'C-47 Skytrain' (USA) and the 'Dakota' (Royal Air Force service). With Russian and Japanese versions built, too, they topped out at over 16,000 in numbers. They were used in the Royal New Zealand Air Force (RNZAF), with 49 aircraft from 1943 to 1977. They were also used extensively in New Zealand's NAC (National Airways Corporation) fleet.

My own introduction to the DC3 was not so great. On 3 July 1963, an NAC Douglas DC3, en route to Tauranga from Auckland, ploughed into the Kaimai Ranges in extremely bad weather with high winds, killing all on board. The plane was found the next day, and 23 bodies were recovered. At the time I was a patrol leader in a Hamilton Scout group, and our scoutmaster, two assistant scoutmasters, our troop leader and the five patrol leaders (including me) hiked into the wreck five weeks after the crash. It was not a pretty sight. It looked as though the pilot had been trying to pull her up, but had sheared the wings off, before she ploughed into a rocky outcrop. The cockpit was unrecognisable, the main body of the fuselage had sheared off behind the cockpit, and was crumpled, not in length, but in circumference, and fire had obviously swept through the inside of it. The tail section had snapped off, and the complete tail section, with the last two seats and the flight attendant's seat, still intact and whole, was about 50 metres further down the ravine, as were the wings. We found one of the engines further down still. Rumour had it, at the time, that a male passenger in the rear seat actually

survived the crash, got out and got beyond the wreck, before sitting under a tree, where he passed away. I have never forgotten that scene. I was just 13 years old at the time.

The venerable old DC3 continued on in our skies into the 1970s. Some of them also became topdressing aircraft. Despite the accident described, they actually had an excellent safety record around the world. Maybe they will be the first and only airliner to hit 100 years' continual service; after all, they have been flying now for 80 years.

Around the world, it is estimated that approximately 400 DC3s are still flying today. So far as I am aware, in New Zealand we have two still flying: one running and registered as an airliner with Air Chathams, the other attached to the Warbirds Association. Both can be accessed by the public for rides or charters, and both are beautifully restored and maintained. There are also other static examples in New Zealand.

The DC3 attached to the Warbirds is privately owned by a syndicate of 38 people. In 2007, she was repainted from a green colour to her current livery. In doing so, she accurately reflects the DC3s of both the RNZAF and the NAC, as many of the NAC Dakotas still had the airforce markings as well as *NAC* on the side. She was also refurbished inside, with Air New Zealand donating business-class fabric for the seats. I had the chance of going aboard her in Whitianga, and with her interior décor it is like stepping back in time 50 years. However, this DC3 is not ex-RNZAF. It was built in 1944, and was reputedly used as personal transport for General MacArthur of the US Army. After the war, she ended up as an airliner with a Philippines airline. Following that, she served as a bush plane in the Australian outback, before ending up in a museum. The syndicate bought her from the Australian museum some 27 years ago. Watching her take off and fly brings back nostalgic memories of times past.

At Wigram's Air Force Museum, we saw an original static-display RNZAF DC3. This one had been decked out to carry Queen Elizabeth II on her 1953 New Zealand tour. We were allowed inside, and to our amazement it was like stepping into a time-warp. For 1953 it would have been the height of luxury, with leather seats with dinette settings, a large ensuite, and all beautifully made and topped off with stunning varnished timberwork.

At the recent Warbirds Over Wanaka airshow, both airworthy DC3s were on hand and flying, and we were fortunate to capture both in flight together with the camera lens. What a great sight to see two of these old iconic birds gracefully flying above the airfield!

The second DC3 carries the luxury Skyliner specifications (as she did in the 1960s), and is owned by Craig and Marion Emeny of Air Chathams. This aircraft was built in 1945, and her delivery trip was to Hamilton, New Zealand, where she was handed over to the RNZAF. This aircraft has had an incredible history, which is presented in detailed form on the Air Chathams website. The aircraft is the last RNZAF DC3 still flying and the last of the NAC fleet still flying, and is the only DC3 still in frontline service in New Zealand.

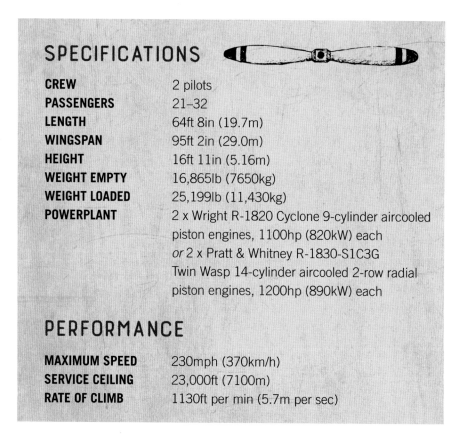

SPECIFICATIONS

CREW	2 pilots
PASSENGERS	21–32
LENGTH	64ft 8in (19.7m)
WINGSPAN	95ft 2in (29.0m)
HEIGHT	16ft 11in (5.16m)
WEIGHT EMPTY	16,865lb (7650kg)
WEIGHT LOADED	25,199lb (11,430kg)
POWERPLANT	2 x Wright R-1820 Cyclone 9-cylinder aircooled piston engines, 1100hp (820kW) each *or* 2 x Pratt & Whitney R-1830-S1C3G Twin Wasp 14-cylinder aircooled 2-row radial piston engines, 1200hp (890kW) each

PERFORMANCE

MAXIMUM SPEED	230mph (370km/h)
SERVICE CEILING	23,000ft (7100m)
RATE OF CLIMB	1130ft per min (5.7m per sec)

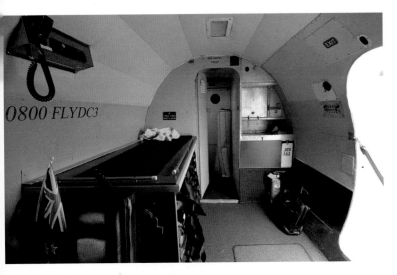

REARWIN SPORTSTER 9000L

1937

In 1928, a businessman by the name of Andrew (Rae) Rearwin decided to create a company to build aircraft. Rae was not a pilot or an aircraft engineer, but he decided he had enough business acumen to be successful. Along with his sons, Ken and Royce, they hired some aircraft engineers and designed and built their first aircraft. The business was domiciled in Kanas, USA.

The first aircraft was a two-seater biplane called the Rearwin KenRoyce, so named for his sons. This was followed by the Rearwin Junior, a high-wing monoplane. Of these first two models, only one of each is believed to exist today. In 1934, a model called the Speedster was designed, but some inherent weaknesses delayed its manufacture and only 11 were built.

Their most successful model was the Rearwin Sportster. The first model variant was known as the '7000', and first flew in 1935. It was a tandem-seat, high-wing monoplane. It was generally powered by a LeBlond 5DE or 5E radial engine. In 1937, Rearwin bought out LeBlond, thus securing the engines for themselves. The company brought out a few more aircraft models before selling out to the Commonwealth Aircraft Company in 1942.

The plane featured here is a 1937 Rearwin Sportster 9000L variant, and was the last and most powerful Sportster model. This aircraft is fitted with the LeBlond 5-cylinder radial engine and develops around 90hp. These little aircraft cruise at around 90–95 miles per hour.

The owner, Tim, is an aircraft engineer. The son of a farmer who was an avid private pilot and collector of aircraft, Tim has been around aircraft since he was a lad. His father had an airstrip and hangar on the farm. This Rearwin is believed to have been imported as a brand-new aircraft by the New Plymouth Aero Club in 1937. Tim's father bought her in 1977, and she has been in the family ever since.

At the time we saw this little honey, Tim was getting close to completing a total restoration on her. Besides restoring this fabric-bodied Rearwin Sportster 9000L, Tim also has two further restorations waiting to be worked on — one is the first Tiger Moth to be registered in New Zealand, and the other, the very first production-built Moth Minor. At the moment, Tim believes there are only around eight Moth Minors flying in the world.

Back to the Rearwin Sportster: from what research we can find, it appears that approximately 260 aircraft were built in their various variants, those being the 7000, 8500 and 9000L.

SPECIFICATIONS

SEATS	2 in tandem
LENGTH	22ft 3in (6.78m)
WINGSPAN	35ft 0in (10.67m)
HEIGHT	6ft 9in (2.06m)
WING AREA	166sqft (15.42sqm)
WEIGHT EMPTY	830lb (376kg)
WEIGHT LOADED	1410lb (640kg)
POWERPLANT	1 x LeBlond 5F radial engine, 90hp (67kW)

PERFORMANCE

MAXIMUM SPEED	118mph (190km/h)
RANGE	480 miles (772km)
SERVICE CEILING	15,200ft (4635m)

RYAN STM and PT22 MONOPLANES

1937

The Ryan STM and PT22 low-wing monoplanes essentially look the same to a layperson. One of each is located at Ardmore aerodrome. Another, in private ownership, is domiciled at Omaka in Blenheim. First designed in 1935 as a sport trainer, they were quickly looked at as a military trainer. In 1936, the STA appeared with an uprated motor, a 150hp supercharged Menasco. In 1937, the Mexican Air Force ordered six Ryan STAs. They were redesignated 'STM' (Sports Trainer Military), and had slightly wider cockpits to allow for pilots to wear parachutes. Soon the US military became interested.

With the Menasco not performing so well in the reliability stakes, given the daily demands of the military, Ryan began looking at other options. They tried a 132hp Kinner radial engine, with the model designated the 'PT20'. Ryan then finetuned the PT20 by lengthening the fuselage and giving it a wider, more circular profile to match the radial engine. With demand for their trainer growing, Ryan upgraded the motor to a 160hp Kinner. The new-engined aircraft were known as the 'PT22' variant.

One of the Ryan STMs in New Zealand is owned by the Museum of Transport and Technology (MOTAT), and is on long-term loan to Warbirds New Zealand, who are responsible for keeping her airworthy and flying her. Apparently, she was in the East Indies, and flew out to Australia just ahead of the Japanese invasion during the war.

The PT22 that is domiciled at Ardmore is definitely the more striking of the two aircraft, sporting a polished aluminium fuselage. This one was manufactured in 1941. She was restored in the United States and flown to the Oshkosh airshow in 1994. She was purchased at Oshkosh by Les Marshal and imported to New Zealand, being registered in 1996 and flown for the first time in New Zealand airspace in 1998.

Both Ryans can be seen at Ardmore with the Warbirds Association. The third, another STM, is owned by Noel Kruse, and is also a most glamorous aircraft, with a stunning polished aluminium fuselage and incredible-looking wheel spats. Again, these aircraft are almost Art Deco in appearance — I love the look of them, and was attracted to them the minute I laid eyes on them.

SPECIFICATIONS

1937 Ryan STM

CREW	2 (instructor and student)
LENGTH	22ft 5in (6.83m)
WINGSPAN	30ft 1in (9.17m)
HEIGHT	6ft 10in (2.08m)
WEIGHT EMPTY	1081lb (490kg)
WEIGHT MAX. TAKEOFF	1860lb (844kg)
POWERPLANT (Original)	1 x Menasco C-4S engine, 150hp (110kW)
(Replacement)	1 x LOM Prague M332A 4-cylinder inline engine, 140hp (103kW)

PERFORMANCE

MAXIMUM SPEED	160mph (258km/h)
RANGE	352 miles (566km)
SERVICE CEILING	17,200ft (5243m)
RATE OF CLIMB	800ft (244m) per min

1941 Ryan PT22

CREW	2 (instructor and student)
LENGTH	22ft 5in (6.83m)
WINGSPAN	30ft 1in (9.17m)
HEIGHT	6ft 10in (2.08m)
WEIGHT EMPTY	1308lb (593kg)
WEIGHT MAX. TAKEOFF	1860lb (844kg)
POWERPLANT	1 x Kinner R-0540-1 radial engine, 160hp (118kW)

PERFORMANCE

MAXIMUM SPEED	131mph (211km/h)
RANGE	352 miles (566km)
SERVICE CEILING	15,500ft (4725m)
RATE OF CLIMB	710ft (216m) per min

The NEW
RYAN

G. BY
ONAUTICAL CO.
GO - CALIF.

ER. No. 492
URED 1940

▼S-56

ROYAL NETHERLANDS
EAST INDIES NAVAL
AIR SERVICE
JAVA 1941-42

ZK-ABC

U.S. ARMY PT-22
AIR CORPS SERIAL
NO. 41-20653
CREW WEIGHT 380 LB

DONATED BY: R. Field

GRAHAM ORPHAN AND *CLASSIC WINGS*: THE MAN, THE MAGAZINE, THE HANGAR

This part of the book was not in the original plan, but really needed to be included. I booked an appointment with Graham Orphan, mainly to see his Fokker Triplane as I wanted to write about the fact that we have eight in New Zealand. I also knew that Graham owned and edited the *Classic Wings* magazine, so I didn't know quite what my reception would be. However, I needn't have been worried. Graham is one of these individuals who has a lifelong love of old aeroplanes — loves flying them, loves collecting and restoring them, loves writing about them, loves promoting them, and loves talking vintage aircraft to anyone who's willing to listen. Above all, he loves the people who are inspired to partake in the sport and fly these wonderful machines. I was privileged to spend a good part of an afternoon with him.

Graham is an imported Aussie, who married a Kiwi girl (good choice). As a boy, Graham was introduced to a Tiger Moth that his father had bought to restore. A move from Adelaide to Brisbane saw the Tiger sold off. Graham was devastated. While still in Adelaide, there was another old vintage plane, a Percival Proctor Mk.I, in a compound at Parafield Airport, which as a boy he would play on. He decided that when he grew up he would buy her and restore her. Unfortunately, she was deemed unsafe and she was given to the airfield fire service, who burnt her. Again, Graham was devastated. He became very worried that by the time he grew up there would be no old planes left to restore. As a teenager, while still at school, he and his mate Pete managed to purchase an old Auster and a wrecked Tiger Moth out of Tully in North Queensland. The aircraft cost them $950 and, with the money they had saved by working their backsides off in the weekends and after school, at any job available, they had just enough left to freight them the

1000 miles home. This was 1974. The planes were stored in a large shed at Pete's place. They decided to restore the Auster first, as she appeared to be in much better condition. However, the boys soon found out that there was a lot more to restoring the aircraft than they had first thought. They decided that it would take years to restore both planes, so, as they liked the Tiger Moth more, they sold off the Auster. Funds restored, they started on their two-year Tiger Moth restoration. Eight years later, she was finished. During those years the boys both learned to fly, bought an airworthy Auster, and met the girls they would each subsequently marry. Sounds like a pretty full-on eight years! Graham sold his share out to another friend, Rob McCann, when he left Brisbane, but continued to fly her when he visited, with Pete flying Graham's planes in Blenheim on return visits. As time passed, the Tiger was sold so that Pete and Rob could buy something they could carry family in. So what happened to the Tiger Moth? She ended up in Blenheim at Omaka, in a syndicate Graham formed to make a home for the aircraft on this side of the Tasman. As Graham is a member, he still gets to fly her, and from his office window in his hangar he often sees other syndicate members taking her for a flight. How cool is that!

For a number of years, Graham talked about starting up a *Classic Wings* magazine. His wife, Jane, finally had enough and said to Graham, 'Look, either start the magazine or shut up about it!' So was born the *Classic Wings* magazine in 1994. Over the past two years, I have been buying these magazines, which are well presented and very informative. There is great photography, and in my journey on this book the magazines have been very helpful. The items in the magazine are for all levels, appealing to the layperson as much as to the enthusiast as much as to the professional. That is a hard ask for any publication to cover, but Graham does it extremely well.

Graham's hangar was also an eye-opener. Besides the Fokker Dr.1 Dreidecker (Triplane), he also has an airworthy Nieuport 11 World War I replica, a 1930s Fleet Finch twin-cockpit biplane, a Boeing Stearman biplane (all owned by Graham and Jane) and a friend's airworthy Mk 14 Spitfire stored there. Besides these airworthy craft, Graham showed me the wood-and-steel-tube-framed fuselage of a 1930s Fairchild, a luxury Art Deco-styled aircraft for four. They even came with windup windows. Stored around the hangar were most of the parts to fully restore her. Up against one wall were the remains of a stripped-down P-40K Kittyhawk: a future restoration? This really is a Man Cave with some serious toys!

As Graham rattled off the names of other iconic and vintage aircraft either existing or being restored or reproduced in the environs of Omaka, I realised just what a hub for rare and vintage aircraft the area is, which in turn means there are an awful lot of dedicated vintage aircraft people also residing in the area. 'And they', says Graham, 'are what makes it all worthwhile.'

WARBIRDS OF THE 1930S AND 1940S

The war had finished only five years prior to my birth. My oldest sister was born in 1945, while my dad was still in the air force, with one of his brothers in England flying Lancasters, and another in the army, having lived through the North Africa and Italy campaigns. So for us kids growing up, World War II was not that far in the past, and was quite close to home, as it would have been to most New Zealand families of the time.

Having a dad and an uncle who had been in the air force was enough to fire up the imagination of their young son and nephew. Undoubtedly, they knew nothing of this, but by the time I was eight I could pretty well tell you the names of the fighters and bombers of both the Allies and the Luftwaffe. I could recite every rank in the Royal Air Force, and its equivalent rank in the army and Royal Navy.

This interest was further enhanced every year on holiday at Long Bay, in the Coromandel. A group of families (including ours) would meet there every year and thoroughly enjoy each other's company for four weeks. Both parents and kids got on wonderfully. One of the kids, Ken, came from Auckland, and he and I were great mates. Ken always brought down heaps of war comics, which he and I would devour on wet days in his parents' caravan awning. I loved the flying ones, with comic-book hero Flight Lieutenant 'Rockfist Rogan', Spitfire Pilot, being the best read ever.

As a very small boy, I can remember Dad taking me out to Rukuhia (now Hamilton Airport), where row upon row of Kittyhawks, Corsairs and Hudson bombers had been abandoned after the war. They were eventually sold off and broken up for parts. Cheap old war planes that were no longer needed. In hindsight, what a waste!

These World War II planes had grown up, when compared with the aircraft of the Great War. In New Zealand, we are lucky enough to have a number of what are now very rare aircraft, both in restored static condition in museums, and in airworthy condition and flown regularly with members of the Warbirds Association.

MESSERSCHMITT Bf 108 TAIFUN

1935

New Zealand's sole Messerschmitt Bf 108 Taifun is actually registered as a Nord 1002 Pingouin (Penguin). Why? After the war, France picked up the remaining airframes and built more of them, powering them with a French-built 233hp Renault engine. They were called the 'Nord 1002 Pingouin'. However, this particular aircraft was built in Germany before the plant shut down, so she is actually a genuine Messerschmitt. She was shot down on two occasions in the war, rebuilt and surrendered to the Allies in Belgium in June 1945. After the war, she was exported to America and passed through a few owners before being rebuilt by Piper Aircraft. Here, the original Argus engine was replaced with a Lycoming 300hp. She was painted in military colours in order to appear in a movie, and was later exported to South Africa in 1989. In March 1996, she was imported to New Zealand and now resides at Tauranga Airport.

The 108 was designed back in 1935 as a M.37 low mono-wing all-metal sport aircraft. As they came off the production line, they became known as the 'Bf 108 Messerschmitt'. They proved to be great long-range aircraft, setting some long-distance records.

Elly Beinhorn, a German aviatrix, flew one from Berlin to Constantinople and back again in a day, establishing a name for herself and, quite literally, a name for the Bf 108. She christened the aircraft *Taifun* (Typhoon), and Messerschmitt adopted the name. Such was the success of the aircraft that they brought out a four-seat version the same year.

Its design served as the basis for the legendary Bf 109. It is said that they put the pilot's seat in the back-seat area, hung a big V12 engine in front, and narrowed the fuselage to create the 109.

The 108 is a great little aircraft, and it is very cool to see her done out in German World War II colours and actually flying.

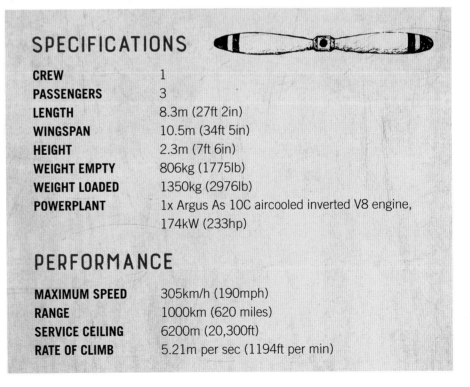

SPECIFICATIONS

CREW	1
PASSENGERS	3
LENGTH	8.3m (27ft 2in)
WINGSPAN	10.5m (34ft 5in)
HEIGHT	2.3m (7ft 6in)
WEIGHT EMPTY	806kg (1775lb)
WEIGHT LOADED	1350kg (2976lb)
POWERPLANT	1x Argus As 10C aircooled inverted V8 engine, 174kW (233hp)

PERFORMANCE

MAXIMUM SPEED	305km/h (190mph)
RANGE	1000km (620 miles)
SERVICE CEILING	6200m (20,300ft)
RATE OF CLIMB	5.21m per sec (1194ft per min)

MESSERSCHMITT Bf 109 (THE INTERLOPER)

1936

In World War II, there seemed to be one iconic fighter that became a legend in each country. In Russia, it was the Yak-3, and in America, the P-51 Mustang. The Brits had the Spitfire, and the Japanese the Mitzubishi Zero. In Germany, it was the Messerschmitt Bf 109 (sometimes known as the 'Me 109').

The star of the Warbirds Over Wanaka 2016 airshow was a Messerschmitt Bf 109. I was at Wanaka and saw this rare and iconic aircraft flying, and in mock battles with her arch enemies, the Spitfire and the Yak-3. What a brilliant aircraft! I thought long and hard about featuring this iconic aeroplane, as she is not domiciled in New Zealand, but was only here for the duration of the airshow. A visitor. An interloper, so to speak. However, she was once owned by New Zealander Ray Hanna, so there are some links.

This one has had the original engine replaced with a V12 Merlin, so she goes very well. The 109 is just one of two flying examples in the world, the other retaining an original engine.

Many of our New Zealand airmen of World War II would have come up against this aircraft, both those in Fighter Command and those in Bomber Command. So in many ways it is quite significant to feature this aircraft. We talk a lot about the various Allied World War II aircraft in this book; not so much about their foes. Hence the featured captured static Zero. To be able to feature both a Japanese Zero and the Messerschmitt 109 — one from the Pacific theatre of war, and one from the European theatre — is just fantastic, and to have all five of these famous fighters featured is really awesome.

The Messerschmitt 109 was first produced in 1936, and was the most produced fighter aircraft in history, with some 33,984 being built, up until April 1945. They were used in the Spanish Civil War, World War II and after the war. They spawned many fighter aces, with the highest-scoring ace of all time, Erich Hartmann of Germany, credited with 352 victories. He also went on to survive the war.

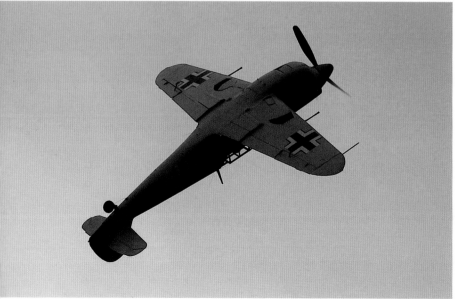

With the 109's low weight and low drag, it was decided to fit the armament in the fuselage. In 1937, the Germans found out that the Brits were fitting guns into the wings of the Hawker Hurricane and Spitfires. To match up, the 109 then received guns in her wings. In 1939, she had a revamp with a complete re-design of the wings, the cooling system and the fuselage aerodynamics.

The 109 was used in the Battle of Britain, but by 1942 it was being replaced on the Western Front by the Focke-Wulf Fw 190. The 109 then continued on at the Eastern Front, the Mediterranean and with the Afrika Korps.

SPECIFICATIONS

CREW	1
LENGTH	8.95m (29ft 7in)
WINGSPAN	9.925m (32ft 6in)
HEIGHT	2.60m (8ft 2in)
WEIGHT EMPTY	2247kg (5893lb)
WEIGHT LOADED	3148kg (6940b)
POWERPLANT	1 x Daimler Benz DB 605A liquid-cooled inverted V12 engine, 1085kW (1455hp) (This example powered by a Rolls Royce Merlin V12.)

PERFORMANCE

MAXIMUM SPEED	640km/h (398mph)
CRUISE SPEED	590km/h (365mph)
RANGE	850km (528 miles)
SERVICE CEILING	12,000m (39,370ft)
RATE OF CLIMB	17.0m per sec (3345ft per min)

ARMAMENT

GUNS	2 x 13mm (.51in) MG 131 machine guns 1 x 20mm (.78in) MG 151/20 cannon
BOMBS	1 x 250kg (551 lb) *or* 4 x 50kg (110lb) bombs
ROCKETS	2 x 21cm (8in) Wfr.Gr. 21 rockets

CATALINA PBY FLYING BOAT

1936

The Catalina PBY flew in its first variation in 1936. They had been designed as a long-range patrol-bomber, but ended up being used in many roles beyond their original brief, including that of air-sea rescue, picking up many downed aircrew in the Pacific theatre.

There were several variations: PBY-1(1936/37), PBY-2 (1937/38), PBY-3 (1938), PBY-4 (1938/39), PBY-5 (1940–43), PBY-5A (1943–45) and PBY-6A (1945). Around 3300 Catalinas were built. They were used mainly for anti-submarine warfare in the Atlantic and Pacific theatres, but also in the Indian Ocean and for escorting convoys to Murmansk.

The Catalinas' parasol wing and large waist blisters afforded excellent visibility, and, along with their long-range ability, made them excellent patrol aircraft. One located the *Bismarck*, leading the Allies to her, and a flight of Catalinas from the Canadian Air Force spotted the Japanese fleet approaching Midway Island. During the war they were also used by the Australians as a commercial passenger plane, flying across the Indian Ocean from Perth to Colombo. The flight took around 30 hours and was made in complete radio silence.

In 1943, the Royal New Zealand Air Force (6 Flying Boat Squadron) used the Catalinas in and around the Pacific, mainly for anti-submarine patrols, operating out of Fiji. They had 22 aircraft.

TEAL, New Zealand's first commercial air passenger line, used former RNZAF Catalinas as survey aircraft for their Coral Routes, which then used Solent flying boats for their passenger service (see page 226).

In New Zealand, we have a Catalina PBY-5A. It is one of only a few remaining airworthy Catalinas in the world. Her call sign is *ZK-PBY*.

Efforts to bring a Catalina to New Zealand ended badly in 1994, when a Canadian-bought Catalina suffered engine failure near Christmas Island on her ferry flight to New Zealand. After an emergency landing, she unfortunately sank. Later that year the syndicate bought and successfully flew another Catalina to New Plymouth. She was a Canadian-built Catalina (1944), and had served with the Canadian Air Force until 1947. She stayed in Canada until 1988, when she was domiciled in South Africa. She was subsequently bought by the New Zealand syndicate and flown 20,000 kilometres to New Zealand, in around 87 hours over four days.

The aircraft was repainted in RNZAF colours, and was seen flying around New Zealand up until just over three years ago. Since then she has undergone an extensive restoration, and made her first restoration test-flight on Friday, 26 February 2016. Her first public appearance was at the 2016 Warbirds Over Wanaka.

Marilyn and I were fortunate enough to be able to spend some time with Brett Emeny and his crew, who have restored the Catalina, on 24 February. We were able to go aboard and photograph and experience this grand old aircraft. Then to see her flying at Wanaka was the icing on the cake. She looks just so stately in the air and on the water. My wife describes her as being so ugly as to be beautiful. If that is possible, then I would have to agree with her.

SPECIFICATIONS

CREW	10 (pilot, co-pilot, bow turret gunner, flight engineer, radio operator, navigator, radar operator, 2 waist gunners, ventral gunner)
LENGTH	63ft 10in (19.4m)
WINGSPAN	104ft 0in (31.70m)
HEIGHT	21ft 1in (6.15m)
WEIGHT EMPTY	20,910lb (9485kg)
WEIGHT LOADED	35,420lb (16,066kg)
POWERPLANT	2 x Pratt & Whitney R-1830-92 twin Wasp radial engines, 1200hp (895kW) each

PERFORMANCE

MAXIMUM SPEED	196mph (314km/h)
CRUISE SPEED	125mph (201km/h)
RANGE	2520 miles (4030km)
SERVICE CEILING	15,800ft (4000m)
RATE OF CLIMB	1000ft per min (5.1m per sec)

ARMAMENT

GUNS	3 x .30cal (7.62mm) machine guns (2 in nose turret, 1 in ventral hatch at tail) 2 x .50cal (12.7mm) machine guns (1 in each waist blister)
BOMBS	4000lb (1814kg) of bombs, *or* depth-charges

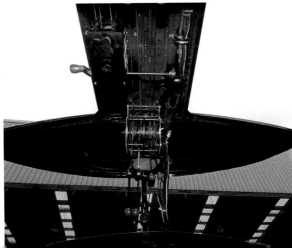

AVRO ANSON

1936

The Avro Anson was a light twin-engined bomber of pre-war manufacture. I always think of the Anson as having a kind of Art Deco appearance. They have elegant lines, and the original cockpit window line is very different. Designed in 1935, they were powered by two Armstrong Siddeley Cheetah IX radial engines producing 350hp each. They were used mainly for reconnaissance and coastal defence. By the time war came, the Anson was used in frontline service on U-boat patrols and around-the-clock bombing, mainly on French ports during the Battle of Britain. As more efficient aircraft came on-stream, the Anson was repositioned for bomber pilot training. In New Zealand, once a pilot had learned to fly a Tiger Moth, they were then designated to Fighter Command or Bomber Command. The Fighter boys trained on the Harvard as their next step, and the Bomber boys on the Avro Anson. New Zealand had only 23 Ansons, so many pilots were posted to Canada to complete their training on Ansons (my uncle, Bob Jessen, among them). From there, they would go to England for advanced training on Oxfords, before conversion to larger bombers.

Bill Reid, owner of the featured Avro Anson, is a renowned helicopter pilot, but has flown fixed-wing aircraft for many years. In his early years he owned a Tiger Moth. He has always had a hankering to own a World War II aircraft, but his favoured Kittyhawk fighter seemed to be on the 'too expensive' list. However, an opportunity arose when Bill spotted an ad in *Classic Wings* magazine: the Airworld Museum in Wangaratta, near Melbourne, was having a closing-down sale. Up for grabs was a modified Avro Anson Mk 1. If Bill had foreseen what was going to become known by the family as the 'Anson affair', he probably would have got a Kittyhawk fighter instead. The Anson was in a sorry state when Bill first saw her, but Bill realised he wanted to restore her back to her original splendour. It took Bill and his volunteer helpers 10 years to reconvert her back to original — and obviously a truck-load of money.

The job that has been done is absolutely outstanding, and the detail of vintage fittings — right down to the engine crank-handles, the original radio, the bomb sights, the bomb racks, the old navigator maps, even the cane basket that a homing pigeon was carried in. (The pigeon was carried in case they had to take to a rubber dinghy: after ditching, they would set the pigeon free to carry their position back to base.) The list of original restored fittings (including a machine gun for the turret) is phenomenal. I was totally blown away with the restoration of this aircraft. She is absolutely unique. Like my Uncle Bob, Bill's father had also trained on Ansons in Canada, and this was part of the attraction for Bill.

This particular Anson was manufactured in 1943 and shipped directly to Australia as a trainer. Not only was she used as a trainer, but she also spent some time on anti-submarine patrols.

Bill has written a book called *Born to Fly*, which recounts his amazing career, mainly in helicopters, but also includes a detailed section on the Anson restoration. The whole book is a great read, and I certainly became quite engrossed in it. Highly recommended reading.

To watch the old Anson in the air is just great. Because she is so different from any other warbird, she attracts attention both in the air and on the ground. She is a brilliant addition to New Zealand's iconic and vintage aircraft fleet.

SPECIFICATIONS

CREW	4 (pilot, navigator/bomb-aimer, radio operator, gunner)
LENGTH	42ft 3in (12.88m)
WINGSPAN	56ft 6in (17.22m)
HEIGHT	13ft 1in (3.99m)
WEIGHT EMPTY	5512lb (2500kg)
WEIGHT LOADED	7955lb (3608kg)
POWERPLANT	2 x Armstrong Siddeley Cheetah IX 7-cylinder radial engines, 350hp (261kW) each

PERFORMANCE

MAXIMUM SPEED	188mph (302km/h)
RANGE	790 miles (1271km)
SERVICE CEILING	19,000ft (5791m)
RATE OF CLIMB	750ft per min (3.8m per sec)

ARMAMENT

GUNS	1 x .303 (7.7mm) machine gun in front fuselage
	1 x .303 (7.7mm) Vickers K machine gun in dorsal turret
BOMBS	360lb (163kg) maximum payload

FIESELER
Fi 156 STORCH
1937 (REPLICA)

The Fieseler Fi 156 went into production first in 1937, and continued on through to 1945. They were famous for their ability to perform short takeoffs and landings. (In aviation circles, this is known as 'STOL performance'.) A design feature, rare for a land-based aircraft, was the ability to fold the wings back along the fuselage so that the aircraft could be trailered. The long legs of the main landing gear were oil-filled, allowing the aircraft to land on relatively rough surfaces. Their appearance gave the Fieseler the look of a long-legged bird, hence the nickname '*Storch*' (which is German for 'stork'), which kind of stuck. Around 2900 Storches were built in Germany. They were also built in France from 1944, after France's liberation. In France, before the war ended, 141 were built, and a total of 925 were built before production ceased in 1965.

During the war the Germans used the Fieseler in the European and North Africa theatres, but the aircraft's two most famous roles were the rescue of Mussolini from a boulder-strewn mountain-top, and the landing in the Tiergarten near the Brandenburg Gate by Hanna Reitsch during the death throes of the Battle of Berlin. Both events demonstrated the Storch's STOL abilities extremely well.

Post-war, the Fieseler was used by the French Army's Light Aviation division in the Indochina War and the Algerian War (1945–1958). There are just eight survivors; however, a number of replicas have been built, mostly to three-quarter scale.

Our featured Storch replica is a three-quarter-scale designed and built in Serbia. She was imported and assembled in New Zealand, and currently resides at Waharoa, Matamata. The aircraft is owned by Angus Robson, who also pilots the aircraft. I spoke with Peter Ryan of Matamata, who often flies this Slepcev Storch replica. Peter says she is amazing to fly, is highly manoeuvrable and, because of her scaled size, weight and engine power, she actually pretty much replicates the performance of the larger original Storch. He can do tight 360-degree turns with the wings level. Now that is something pretty special. She also has an amazing climb angle of attack once in the air. (See the photograph.) The replica is powered by a 100hp Rotax engine. For a replica, she looks very authentic, and a lot of work has gone into the canopy glazing. She is just a sweet little aircraft that really catches the eye.

SPECIFICATIONS

CREW	1
LENGTH	9.9m (32ft 6in)
WINGSPAN	14.3m (46ft 9in)
HEIGHT	3.1m (10ft 0in)
WEIGHT EMPTY	860kg (1900lb)
WEIGHT LOADED	1260kg (2780lb)
POWERPLANT	1 x Argus As 10 aircooled V8 engine, 180kW (240hp)

PERFORMANCE

MAXIMUM SPEED	175km/h (109mph)
RANGE	380km (240 miles)
SERVICE CEILING	4600m (15,090ft)
RATE OF CLIMB	4.8m per sec (945ft per min)

1937 Slepcev Storch (replica)

LENGTH	24ft 4in (7.42m)
WINGSPAN	34ft 10in (10.6m)
HEIGHT	9ft 6in (2.9m)
WEIGHT EMPTY	640lb (290kg)
WEIGHT LOADED	1200lb (544kg)
POWERPLANT	1 x Rotax 912ULS engine, 100hp (75kW)

PERFORMANCE

MAXIMUM SPEED	93mph (150km/h)
CRUISE SPEED	83 mph (133km/h)
STALL SPEED	25mph (40km/h)
RANGE	365 miles (587.4km)
SERVICE CEILING	13,500ft (4115m)
RATE OF CLIMB	6m per sec (1200ft per min)

AIRSPEED OXFORD

1937

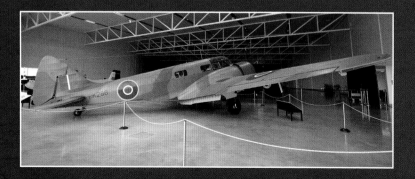

The Airspeed Oxford was built as an advanced trainer in 1937 for bomber aircrews. They had dual controls for pilot training, and were set up for training navigators. The co-pilot's seat could be moved back to be level with the navigation table for navigator training, at the same time creating a space to train bomb-aimers. Behind the cockpit bulkhead was a wireless operator's position. A turret was fitted for air-to-air gunnery. Before long they developed the Mk1 and Mk2, both being configured slightly differently to suit training needs. A total of 8586 Oxfords were built.

The Oxford was the preferred trainer for the Empire Air Training Scheme. Many were sent to Canada, along with many aircrews from all over the Empire (including New Zealand) for training. Actual planes were also sent to Australia, South Africa and New Zealand. The Royal New Zealand Air Force (RNZAF) had 299 Airspeed Oxfords (Mk1 and Mk2 models) during World War II. Over 100 were based at Wigram alone. They were primarily a trainer for pilots and crew, who would progress on to Wellington bombers. They were used for all types of advanced aircrew training. The Mk1s came with a dorsal turret, while the Mk2, supposedly used for advanced pilot training, did not have one. However the RNZAF was pretty good at modifying aircraft, so ours had a mix of turrets across the Marks. During their tenure with the RNZAF, six were modified to Consul configuration for freight- and passenger-carrying. This was done between 1948 and 1952. In 1944, large numbers were put into storage at Woodbourne, with 112 being sold off in 1947. Seventy-six were written-off in accidents, and another 36 were scrapped because of deterioration.

The restored Oxford on static display at Wigram was built by Airspeed Limited as an Oxford Mk1, for the RAF. Her serial number is *PK286*. She saw little service, and was sold back to Airspeed for a civil conversion to Consul status. In this form she was registered as *G-AIKR* in 1946. She was purchased in 1947 by Airwork Ltd, and in 1962 passed to the Rapid Flying Group. After failing an airworthiness certificate in 1965, she was destined to become a children's playground attraction (a fate that befell many World War II aircraft), but

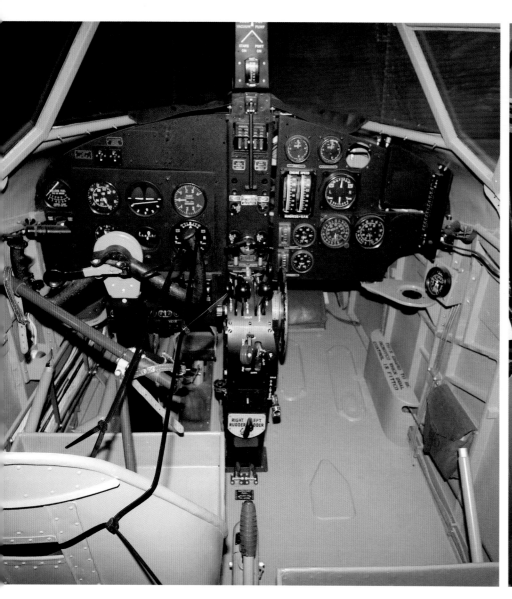

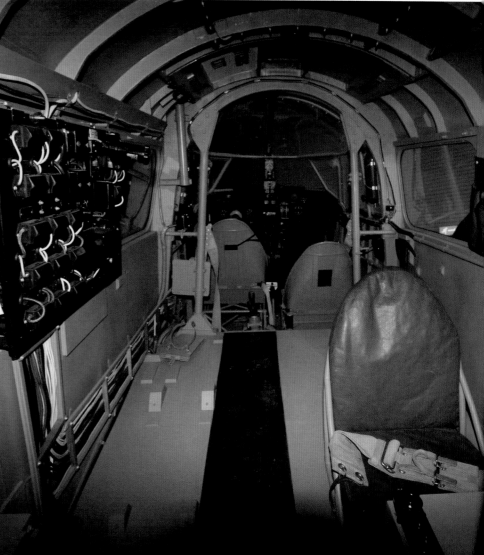

was rescued by the Canadian Aviation and Space Museum and placed in storage. In late 2000, the Air Force Museum of New Zealand (at Wigram) arranged for a long-term loan, receiving the aircraft in 2001.

The Oxford is mainly built of wood and fabric. She has been restored to her original Mk1 Oxford specifications. This required removing the Consul-style cabin windows and replacing them with Oxford-type windows, removing the seats and fore and aft cabin bulkheads, and reinstalling bomb bays and turret fittings. The 'Consul' elongated nose was removed, and the perspex bomb-aimer's nose was constructed and refitted. The workmanship right through this project has been of a very high standard, and once again I am reminded of the talented engineers and craftsmen we have in the New Zealand aviation area. The finished restoration is as historically genuine as it can possibly be, and is a credit to the dedicated team at the museum who carried out the restoration.

We were very fortunate to be able to step inside this aircraft and experience her, as well as photograph the interior.

While writing this I came to realise that I have now experienced four of the five aircraft that my Uncle Bob flew in the war — the Tiger Moth, the Avro Anson, the Airspeed Oxford (see accompanying photograph of my uncle at the controls in 1944) and the Lancaster. The only one missing from the line-up is the Wellington bomber. It has been so interesting finding links to family history along the journey of writing this book.

SPECIFICATIONS

CREW	3
LENGTH	34ft 6in (10.52m)
WINGSPAN	53ft 4in (16.26m)
HEIGHT	11ft 1in (3.38m)
WEIGHT EMPTY	5322lb (2419kg)
WEIGHT LOADED	7500lb (3409kg)
POWERPLANT	2 x Armstrong Siddeley Cheetah X radial engines, 350hp (261kW) each

PERFORMANCE

MAXIMUM SPEED	192mph (309 km/h)
ENDURANCE	5.5 hr
SERVICE CEILING	23,550ft (7108m)
RATE OF CLIMB	1340ft per min (6.8m per sec)

ARMAMENT

GUNS	0.303in (7.7mm) Vickers K machine gun in dorsal turret
BOMBS	16 x 11.5lb (5kg) practice bombs

NORTH AMERICAN HARVARD

1937

According to the research I have carried out, and cross-checked and double-checked, as far as I am aware 202 North American Harvard advanced air trainers were delivered to the Royal New Zealand Air Force (RNZAF) between 1941 and 1944. As we have learned, our trainee pilots got their wings in a Tiger Moth, and were then designated to either Bomber Command or Fighter Command. While many of those who followed the Bomber route were shipped off to Canada to train on Avro Ansons, the Fighter boys went to train in the Harvards. This was the next step on the way to flying a true Fighter aircraft, such as the Kittyhawk or, later in the war, the Corsair. If shipped to England, then it was the precursor to the Hurricane or the Spitfire. Production on the Harvard started in 1937.

After the war, the majority of RNZAF Harvards were put into storage in late 1945. Many were apparently sold for scrap around 1958/59. The remaining Harvards were modernised between 1955 and 1957, and used as trainers. In 1977, the last 19 airworthy Harvards, along with another 13 in storage, were withdrawn from service and sold off. Some of these aircraft were to form the nucleus of the Warbirds Association's aircraft. It is believed that five Harvards remain with the air force: two are reserve aircraft with the RNZAF Historic Flight, stored at Ohakea, one is on display at Wigram Air Force Museum, another is the gate guardian at the museum, and the fifth one is with the Historic Flight but is an airworthy example.

According to the 2015 Civil Aviation Authority register, there are another 15 airworthy Harvards flying our skies. At the shows and fly-ins I have attended over the past two years, there always appear to be five or six Harvards present, with up to nine at one Warbirds open day. These tandem two-seater trainers look like a World War II fighter, have their own distinctive sound, and are powered by a 9-cylinder Pratt & Whitney Wasp R-1340 supercharged radial engine, producing 600hp.

They are highly aerobatic, and came to fame in New Zealand with the RNZAF Red Checkers Aerobatic Display Team. That fame is now continued with the outstanding Warbirds 'Roaring Forties' Aerobatic Display Team.

I love watching these old Harvards (which are called 'Texans' in the United States). I have got to know about eight or nine of them now, and am getting to recognise them by their colour schemes and numbers, and gradually learning who the pilots are and which one they fly. I love their sound, their looks and, most of all, I love watching them carry out aerobatic manoeuvres, especially the Roaring Forties team as they go through their formation aerobatics. Having flown all those years ago, I have a sound respect for those who do aerobatics, and even more so for those who carry out formation aerobatics. That is a whole new level of pilot skill.

Enjoy the photo images of New Zealand's iconic North American Harvards that we have managed to put together.

Three individual Harvard histories

ZK-TVI (civil registration) or *NZ 1057* (RNZAF registration) is one of the 202 aircraft of this type delivered to the Royal New Zealand Air Force in the 1940s. She was disposed of in 1977, like many others, and was bought for a children's playground amusement. Let's hope she actually inspired some children to go on to become pilots when they grew up! She was recovered from this rather sad and undignified end, and subsequently was rebuilt, from the wheels up, to flying condition in 1998. She is presented in her 1950s RNZAF livery. This aircraft is registered to Warbird Adventure Rides Ltd, which is owned and operated by Liz Needham and Frank Parker, both highly experienced pilots. This particular Harvard is owned and mainly flown by Liz. Besides being able to experience a ride in this plane with Liz, you can also see her piloting the plane as part of the Roaring Forties aerobatic team.

ZK-ENF (civil registration) or *NZ 1065* (RNZAF registration) is again an ex-RNZAF Harvard, and was disposed of in 1977, too. Unlike *57*, *65* remained a well-maintained flying example, and did not need any restoration. Today, as one of the aerobatic warbirds, she is maintained in original condition. She was initially owned by a syndicate, but, as sometimes happens, the syndicate started to become less interested. At that point, Frank Parker, a syndicate

member, bought the aircraft off the other members of the syndicate. She is now owned by Frank, and shares a hangar with Liz's Harvard and their Kittyhawk. Again available for rides, she is also piloted by Frank in the Roaring Forties aerobatic team. Frank, with this aircraft, is the leader of the team. He jokes that he has the easiest job in the team, as everyone else has to hold formation with him. Having watched them perform several times, I am not sure that he is right about that!

ZK-ENA (civil registration) *NZ 1037* (RNZAF registration) is also an ex-RNZAF Harvard, and arrived in New Zealand in 1943 and was assembled at Hobsonville. She was allocated to the RNZAF's Central Flying School in Tauranga, in 1944. From 1950 until 1955, she served with 2 Territorial Squadron, before being allocated to Ohakea. She was one of the Harvards that were upgraded in the mid-1950s. By the early 1970s, she was in use as a forward air control (FAC) aircraft. During her 34-year career with the RNZAF, she was involved in three ground incidents. In 1945 she collided with *1024* while taxiing, in 1952 her wingtip connected with a hangar in Ohakea, and in 1956 she managed to collide with a marker light at Whenuapai. Declared surplus to requirements by the government in 1977, she was sold to J. Matheson, of Ranfurly, Otago, in 1978. In 1997, W. Matheson bought her; and in 2005 she was bought by Ray Hanna, John Lamont and Brendon Deere, all well-known in New Zealand historic aircraft circles, and all very proficient pilots in their own right.

SPECIFICATIONS

CREW	2
LENGTH	28ft 11in (8.59m)
WINGSPAN	42ft 0in (12.81m)
HEIGHT	11ft 8in (3.57m)
WEIGHT EMPTY	4158lb (1886kg)
WEIGHT LOADED	5617lb (2548kg)
POWERPLANT	1 x Pratt & Whitney Wasp R-1340–AN-1 9-cylinder radial engine, 600hp (450kW)

PERFORMANCE

MAXIMUM SPEED	208mph (335km/h)
RANGE	730 miles (1175m)
SERVICE CEILING	24,200ft (7400m)
RATE OF CLIMB	1200ft per min (6.1m per sec)

ARMAMENT

Provision for up to 3 x .30cal (7.62mm) machine guns

ROARING FORTIES AEROBATIC DISPLAY TEAM

This team of amazing pilots has been thrilling audiences around the country for a number of years. Their Harvards are all ex-Royal New Zealand Air Force aircraft, and all of them wear their original Air Force number painted on the fuselage. A short profile on each of the pilots currently on the team gives a little insight into the aviation background of each member of this highly talented team. The usual aerobatic aircraft are featured here in identification photographs, but sometimes other Harvards are used in the team.

Frank Parker is the team leader, and flies in number 1 position in his own Harvard, RNZAF No. *NZ 1065* (*ZK-ENF*). Frank has in excess of 15,000 hours' flying time, and is currently an international airline captain with Air New Zealand. He also is the current president of the Warbirds Association. Before flying for Air New Zealand, Frank was with the RNZAF, and flew in the aerobatic Red Checkers team for several years. He was also an instructor on the Sioux and Iroquois helicopters and the CT4 trainer. Frank is rated on the Kittyhawk and Spitfire aircraft as well.

Liz Needham is New Zealand's most experienced woman pilot, having racked up an amazing 25,000-plus hours since 1974. She built up an excellent flying school, and is New Zealand's first A-rated woman instructor. She is also an airline captain for Air New Zealand, flying a Boeing 767. A longtime warbirds enthusiast, she is one of a very select group of women in the world to be rated on both the Kittyhawk and the Spitfire. Married to Frank, she flies in number 2 position in the Roaring Forties aerobatic display team, flying her own Harvard, RNZAF No. *NZ 1057* (*ZK-TVI*).

Rob Sillich is an electrical engineer and holds a private pilot's licence. He has an extensive background in competition and display aerobatics. He also flies other warbirds, including the T28 Trojan aircraft. He flies in number 3 position on the team, in RNZAF No. *NZ 1078* (*ZK-ENG*).

John Kelly is a commercial pilot and flight instructor on both general aircraft and warbird aircraft. He has a background in both competition and display aerobatics. He is also on the Warbirds Association committee, and is the Warbirds' historian. He generally flies number 4 position, in RNZAF No. *NZ 1053* (*ZK-JJA*).

Dave Brown flies number 5 position, and is an airline captain flying for Cathay Pacific. He is also ex-RNZAF, where he flew the Skyhawk, the Strikemaster and the CT4 trainer, the latter two as an instructor. For several years he flew the Strikemaster in solo aerobatic displays for the air force. His Harvard is RNZAF No. *NZ 1052* (*ZK-MJN*). In his spare time, Dave is the chief flying instructor for the Warbirds Association, and still flies both the Strikemaster and the Harvard at airshows.

CURTISS P-40 KITTYHAWK

1938

It's funny how long-forgotten memories have been revived, and how planes that have touched my life in one way or another have emerged from the distant past to re-connect with this book. Two of the four Hudson bombers I have found were serviced by my father in Guadalcanal. They are still around in one form or another, and a De Havilland Rapide in which our family flew over the Southern Alps in 1965 is still flying. My uncle flew a Lancaster that was built in 1945; the Lancaster in the Museum of Transport and Technology (MOTAT) was also built in 1945. I have connected physically with all of these individual aircraft, and they are featured in this book.

My first recollection of the Kittyhawk is seeing a bundle of them lined up at the end of the Rukuhia Airport (now Hamilton Airport) in the mid-1950s. Dad had been stationed there from September 1943 to 1945, after returning from Guadalcanal. In fact, he had been part of the ground crew who parked up the aircraft. So he took the whole family out to see them. They had a number of different aircraft types out there, and over a 10-year period, from 1948 to 1959, the air force sold them all for scrap at scrap prices. The RNZAF had operated a little under 300 Kittyhawks on a lend–lease basis from the Americans between 1942 and 1946.

When I started researching the Kittyhawks that we have in New Zealand, I came across the one domiciled at Hood Aerodrome, and found that she was actually one of the Kittyhawks from Rukuhia! She is an 'E' variant. She had been rescued from Rukuhia in 1959, when Charles Darby (an aircraft restorer) and a group of young lads came up with enough money to buy one. They reputedly grabbed the best one they could that was nearest the gate. She was loaned to MOTAT, where she was restored to static display status. From there she was bought by Ray Hanna, who had her restored over a number of years to airworthiness. She first flew again in 1997. Eventually, ownership transferred to The Old Stick and Rudder Company, and she is now based at Hood Aerodrome.

Having seen these Kittyhawks and wondered about the shark faces painted on them, and seen others in photographs on the internet, I satisfied my curiosity by researching what it was all about. Apparently a 'volunteer' group of American pilots, who were led by a retired American general who had moved to China, made an arrangement with the Chinese Government to fly active service as part of the Chinese Air Force, flying Kittyhawks against the invading Japanese. They called themselves the 'Flying Tigers', and the shark face was painted on all of their aircraft. In a small way they helped the Pacific war by tying up Japanese aircraft and personnel in China.

Our Masterton Kittyhawk is painted in Chinese Nationalist markings, with the Flying Tigers squadron's famous shark face. This shark face is now being copied and applied to other Kittyhawks. I absolutely love it. It just looks so aggressive, and really suits the aircraft.

The second Kittyhawk I came across has quite a different history. This one (registered as *ZK-CAG*) was built in 1943 (an 'N' variant) and served in the Royal Australian Air Force with 75 Squadron under a lend–lease agreement with the Americans, similar to the arrangement New Zealand had. She operated in New Guinea with both 75 and 78 squadrons. In May 1944, she had a major electrical meltdown while in the air, and, after a fairly heavy landing accident, was scrapped and subsequently abandoned in New Guinea. In the mid-1970s, once again to the rescue came Charles Darby. The Kittyhawk was retrieved, and restored to flying condition in Auckland. She made her first public appearance in 2000.

From the 13,000-plus Kittyhawks built, these are 2 of about 12 airworthy examples in the world, although there are other examples under restoration in New Zealand.

The latter Kittyhawk is set up as a two-seater and is available for rides through Warbird Adventure Rides.

I have seen both of these aircraft up close, and have seen *ZK-CAG* flown twice by Warbirds pilot Liz Needham (see page 158). It is fantastic to watch Liz throw this beautiful aeroplane around the sky with apparent ease. I have also seen Liz fly as number 2 in the Roaring Forties Harvard aerobatic team, and I can't quite make up my mind whether she is just an extraordinary pilot or half-bird! This Kittyhawk is registered to Warbird Adventure Rides Ltd, and is owned by husband-and-wife team Frank Parker and Liz Needham.

Recently, I saw the two Kittyhawks flying together, along with other legendary World War II fighter aircraft. What a beautiful sight it was.

SPECIFICATIONS

CREW	1
LENGTH	31.67ft (9.66m)
WINGSPAN	37.33ft (11.38m)
HEIGHT	12.33ft (11.38m)
WEIGHT EMPTY	6070lb (3760kg)
WEIGHT LOADED	8810lb (4000kg)
POWERPLANT	1 x Allison V-1710-39 liquid-cooled V12 engine, 1150hp (858kW)

PERFORMANCE

MAXIMUM SPEED	360mph (580km/h)
RANGE	650 miles (1100km)
SERVICE CEILING	29,000ft (8800m)
RATE OF CLIMB	2100ft per min (11m per sec)

ARMAMENT

GUNS	6 x .50in (12.7mm) M2 Browning machine guns
BOMBS	250–1000lb (110–450kg) bombs to a total of 2000lb (907kg) on 3 hardpoints (1 under fuselage, 2 under wing)

The featured Spitfire is a rare two-seater. She is registered as *ZK-WDQ*. Originally, she was a single-seater built in July 1943. She was a Mark IX with a Merlin 61 engine. She saw combat service initially in 65 Squadron, and saw service with squadrons 229 and 312 through to the end of the war. She flew 89 combat missions in all. After the war she was transferred to Air Services Training, and was fitted with a Merlin 63 engine. She was scrapped in 1948. Using parts from other scrapped Spitfires, she was rebuilt in America, first flying again in November 2006. Here, she was converted to a two-seat configuration, with parts being secured from a genuine two-seater Spitfire that was being converted to a single-seater.

She was bought by Doug Brooker, and arrived in New Zealand in early May 2008. Doug, a well-known New Zealand aerobatic pilot, also pilots the Spitfire, along with a small number of renowned New Zealand Warbirds pilots. Upon arrival, the Spitfire was painted in the desert colours and markings of New Zealand's own highest-scoring ace (27.5 kills) Squadron Leader Colin Gray.

Since 2008, this iconic Spitfire has been seen at airshows around New Zealand, has been written about and generally become quite famous. Under the auspices of Warbird Adventure Rides, you can actually purchase a ride in this iconic aircraft. It would be a ride that most people treasure in memory for the rest of their lives, I would think.

I have now seen this aircraft up close quite a few times, and watched her fly at Ardmore and Tauranga. She never fails to stir the blood, and to watch her fly and listen to the beautiful sound of the Merlin V12 engine is simply uplifting.

SPITFIRE
Mκ IX

1938

The Mk IX Spitfire was the favourite Mark of his uncle's, and the Spitfire has been painted in the correct squadron markings of the Biggin Hill squadron his uncle commanded, and of course bears the personal markings that replicate the exact plane his uncle flew.

The test-flight was carried out by renowned warbird pilot Keith Skilling, and went without a hitch. For the past seven years, she has flown very reliably, needing minimal maintenance.

This particular Spitfire initially served with the Royal Air Force's Mediterranean force, and saw action in Italy and over Yugoslavia. In the early 1950s, she was with the Israeli Air Force, before being sold to the Burmese Air Force as a trainer. She was actually used in combat against Kuomintang guerrillas on the North Eastern border. She was retired in 1956, and sat in storage for a while, before being mounted as a gate guardian.

Brendon also owns a Harvard and an Avenger bomber. The Spitfire is currently flown by Squadron Leader Sean Parrot, RNZAF (Ohakea), a highly experienced pilot who flew in the RAF Red Checkers aerobatic team in the United Kingdom.

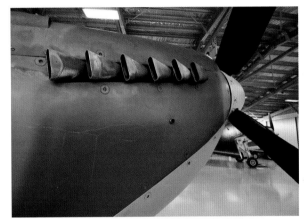

SPECIFICATIONS

CREW	1 or 2
LENGTH	31ft 5in (9.5m)
WINGSPAN	32ft 6in (9.9m)
HEIGHT	12ft 8in (3.86m)
WEIGHT EMPTY	5090lb (2309kg)
WEIGHT LOADED	7400lb (3354kg)
POWERPLANT	1 x Merlin V12 61 or 63 engine, 1560hp (1147kW) or 1690hp (1243kW)

PERFORMANCE

MAXIMUM SPEED	404mph (650km/h)
RANGE	434 miles (698km)
SERVICE CEILING	42,500ft (12,954m)
RATE OF CLIMB	4745ft per min (21.4m per sec)

ARMAMENT

2 x 20mm cannon and 2 x 12.7mm machine guns in the wing

deployed to Palikulo Bay Airfield on Espiritu Santo on 9 October 1942. By 23 November, half of the aircraft of 3(GR) were deployed to Henderson Airfield on Guadalcanal, along with enough ground crew to keep them operational, my father among them. Their brief was long-range reconnaissance, conducting daily and nightly searches to the approaches of Guadalcanal, and low-level searches of the nearby islands. They became the spotters for the American long-range bombers and shorter-range Avenger torpedo bombers. They were ordered not to go hunting enemy aircraft, and to only engage if attacked.

I can remember my father telling me how pressed they were to keep the aircraft airborne, and how the aircrews were flying well beyond what they could manage. After a short time the commanding officer sat down with the Americans and reorganised patrols to what they could manage. Dad organised an operational ride in a Hudson with his crew (as an unauthorised passenger), and on the way home they were jumped by Japanese fighters. In the hands of an experienced pilot, the Hudson could out-turn many a fighter, by feathering the inboard prop and applying maximum power to the outboard prop. Dad said this was how they escaped and evaded the fighters until they were able to get lost in some cloud cover. Imagine my surprise, when researching the Hudsons, to find pretty much the same story recorded on the internet. Hudson *NZ 2049* was among 3(GR) Squadron's first tour, was one of the first to arrive at Guadalcanal, and was the first to see action when she was attacked by Japanese fighters, and survived. The fight apparently lasted some 18 minutes. It was Flying Officer (later Wing Commander) George Gudsell who was the skipper, and who went on to be awarded the Distinguished Flying Cross (US) decoration for his service in this Hudson.

In 2007, the remains of this particular Hudson were bought by Bill Reid, of Wakefield, who plans to restore her for static display. I had the opportunity to see her and climb on board with Bill and my wife, Marilyn. I saw the bullet scars and the patches fitted over some of the bullet holes. It was kind of surreal to realise that this was the aircraft, photographed at the bottom of the opposite page, that my father was in at the time (1942), and that it was likely my father who had patched the bullet scars, along with servicing this aircraft.

There are three other static-display Hudsons in New Zealand. *NZ 2035* is in the hands of Ferrymead Museum. The rebuild of this aircraft continues today. It served in 1(GR) Squadron. One of the two restored static Hudsons featured in this book is *NZ 2013,* based at the Royal New Zealand Air Force museum at Wigram, Christchurch. *NZ 2013* saw action also in 1(GR) Squadron, then in 4(GR) Squadron, in Fiji, along with a short spell in New Caledonia. She then served with the school of navigation and reconnaissance until 1948. The other Hudson, housed at MOTAT in Auckland, served in 3(GR) Squadron, and again at Espiritu Santo and Guadalcanal in her early days. She was later changed to a transport plane, and became the personal plane of Group Captain Geoffrey Roberts, Air Officer commanding 1 Islands Group. There is no doubt that Bill Reid's Hudson and the MOTAT Hudson would have both been worked on by my father, and that Bill Reid's Hudson was the one Dad was in when it got attacked. Talk about ghosts from the past!

The black-and-white photographs, here, show my father and two of the six early Hudsons at Guadalcanal, with the ground crew grouped around the foremost Hudson. My father is sitting by the right-hand wheel.

SPECIFICATIONS

CREW	6 (pilot, navigator, radio operator, flight engineer, gunner, bomb-aimer)
LENGTH	44ft 4in (13.51m)
WINGSPAN	65ft 6in (19.96m)
HEIGHT	11ft 10in (3.62m)
WEIGHT EMPTY	12,000lb (5400kg)
WEIGHT LOADED	17,500lb (7930kg)
WEIGHT MAX. TAKEOFF	18,500lb (8390kg)
POWERPLANT	2 x Wright Cyclone 9-cylinder radial engines, 1100hp (820kW) each

PERFORMANCE

MAXIMUM SPEED	246mph (397 km/h)
RANGE	1960 miles (3150km)
SERVICE CEILING	24,000ft (7470m)
RATE OF CLIMB	1200ft per min (6.2 m per sec)

ARMAMENT

GUNS	2 x .303in (7.7mm) Browning machine guns in dorsal turret
	2 x .303in Browning machine guns in nose
BOMBS	750lb (340kg) payload

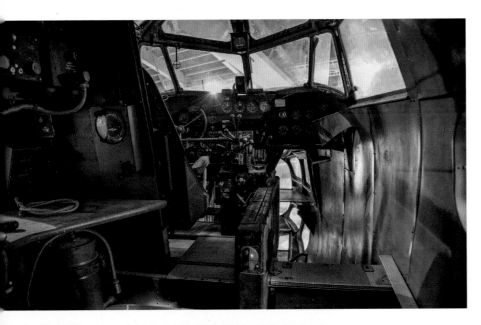

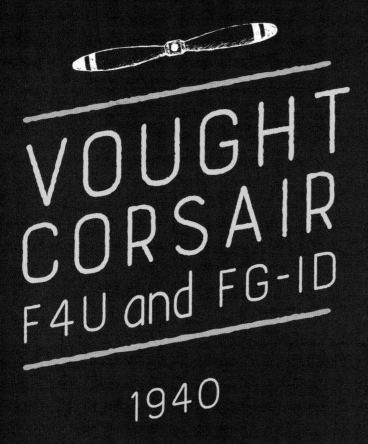

VOUGHT CORSAIR
F4U and FG-ID
1940

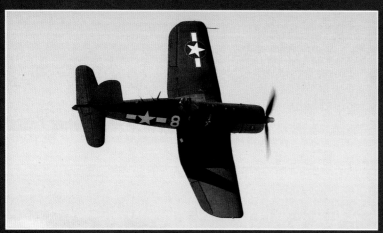

The Corsair was designed in 1939, with the first prototype flying in 1940. With modifications, it was to be 1942 before the first Corsairs rolled off the production line. Primarily designed as aircraft-carrier fighters, they initially proved to be not so good, as visibility was difficult and they had a tendency to bounce on landing. While this was no great problem on land, it was not so good on an aircraft carrier. The Corsair is a distinctive aircraft. They are large for a fighter, they look aggressive, and the gull-wing shape of the wings gives them a menacing look. As such, they tended to be used as a land-based aircraft. From February 1943, Corsairs operated from Guadalcanal in the Solomons, where the Corsair was found to be effective against the Japanese Zero.

The Royal New Zealand Air Force (RNZAF) was equipped with Kittyhawks in the Pacific, and compared with American fighter squadrons they were pretty impressive. Because of this factor, America gave New Zealand early access to the Corsair. Some 424 Corsairs equipped 13 RNZAF squadrons. Most were F4U-1s, with the 'FG-ID' of this particular aircraft denoting which factory she was built in. The first deliveries commenced under the lend–lease programme, in March 1944. By the time they became active, there was virtually no Japanese Air Force or Navy left in the area New Zealand was designated, so the Corsairs were mainly used for ground support for New Zealand soldiers fighting the Japanese.

After the war, they were stored along with Kittyhawks, Hudsons, Avengers and Venturas at the 'Rukuhia graveyard', and were later disposed of. In American hands, the Corsair went on to be a prominent and effective fighter in the Korean conflict.

Of all the Corsairs that went to the graveyard, only one remains in airworthy condition. A Rukuhia garage proprietor, name of J. Asplin, bought up 32 of the Corsairs in 1949 and broke them up. By 1960, only three remained. I can remember Asplin's garage. For many years the tail section of a Corsair was mounted on his garage roof, looking for all the world like it had crashed through the roof!

During the early 1960s, one was restored to static/taxiing condition. She sat at Hamilton Airport for a few years before going on display at MOTAT. Asplin retained ownership, and this RNZAF Corsair was eventually sold into America. An unfortunate set of circumstances saw her unloaded in Canada, where she got caught up in some bureaucratic nonsense when Canada declared her 'an article of war'. By the time she got to the States, she was in a pretty sorry condition. After an 11-year restoration, she flew again. From there, the Corsair ended up in England before returning to New Zealand.

Today she is resplendent in her original RNZAF colours, and resides in Masterton with The Old Stick and Rudder Company.

To watch this bird in flight is breath-taking. Many years ago, I had an ex-RNZAF Corsair World War II pilot working for me, and I loved hearing him talk about the Corsair, so for me to see her in flight is really quite special.

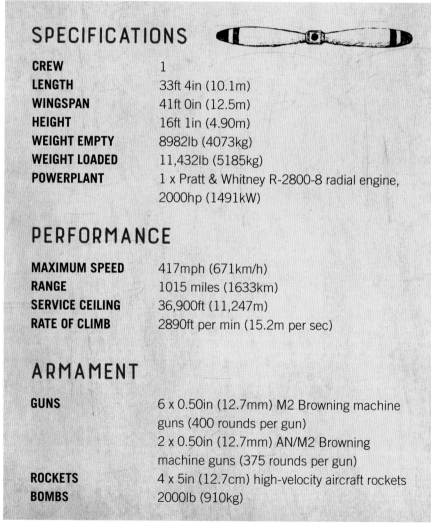

SPECIFICATIONS

CREW	1
LENGTH	33ft 4in (10.1m)
WINGSPAN	41ft 0in (12.5m)
HEIGHT	16ft 1in (4.90m)
WEIGHT EMPTY	8982lb (4073kg)
WEIGHT LOADED	11,432lb (5185kg)
POWERPLANT	1 x Pratt & Whitney R-2800-8 radial engine, 2000hp (1491kW)

PERFORMANCE

MAXIMUM SPEED	417mph (671km/h)
RANGE	1015 miles (1633km)
SERVICE CEILING	36,900ft (11,247m)
RATE OF CLIMB	2890ft per min (15.2m per sec)

ARMAMENT

GUNS	6 x 0.50in (12.7mm) M2 Browning machine guns (400 rounds per gun) 2 x 0.50in (12.7mm) AN/M2 Browning machine guns (375 rounds per gun)
ROCKETS	4 x 5in (12.7cm) high-velocity aircraft rockets
BOMBS	2000lb (910kg)

NORTH AMERICAN MUSTANG P-51D

1940

The P-51D Mustang fighter has always been, in my mind, one of the most iconic fighters of World War II. They were the first fighter fitted with long-range fuel tanks, which enabled them to escort American bombers from England all the way to Berlin and back again, giving the bombers air cover from the German fighters. Apparently, Hitler refused to believe that American fighters were accompanying the bombers! In his mind, it just couldn't be done.

I have always thought that the Mustang was one of the prettiest fighters of the era, too. The Mustang was designed with a prototype produced in just 117 days by the North American aircraft company, after it received a provisional procurement order in early 1940 from the Royal Air Force (RAF) for 320 aircraft. In September, the RAF upped their order to 620 aircraft, with a further increase of another 300 in December. Initially, the Brits specified a 1150hp Allison engine, but, because of a rapid drop-off in power at higher altitudes, it was not as good as it could be.

The first production model came off the line in 1941. From the original order, 93 Mustangs went to Britain. With the attack on Pearl Harbor, further Mustang production was diverted to the US forces. In 1942, three of the British Mustangs were fitted with Rolls Royce Merlin V12 engines, and the increase in performance was amazing. The United States had been fully briefed on the changes, and they subsequently fitted Packard Merlin V12 engines to the Mustang. Large numbers of Mustangs went to the European theatre.

New Zealand's involvement with the Mustang began in August 1945. Under its lend–lease arrangement with the United States, New Zealand was to receive 370 Mustangs. After the first 30 arrived, the war ended, and so the balance of the order was cancelled. The 30 were promptly mothballed, until being reinstated with the territorial forces in 1951. They were withdrawn in 1955, and sold for scrap in 1958, with most of them having their wings torched off.

One of the Mustangs featured here has been in New Zealand since 1984, when she was imported by Sir Tim Wallis. She had been built in 1944 and served with the Royal Canadian Air Force. When later Sir Tim wanted to sell her to purchase a Spitfire, a trust was set up to keep her in New Zealand. The Mustang is kept at Ardmore in the Warbirds Museum when she is not flying. From there, she passed to an Ardmore-based syndicate, before being bought by Graham Bethell. The Mustang is a regular at the airshows, and is available for rides — what a brilliant aircraft to go for a flight in. I have watched this aircraft in flight several times now, often in the company of the Ardmore-based Kittyhawk and Spitfire. What a fantastic trio they make.

The other Mustang featured is Wanaka-based, and has the name *Dove of Peace* written down the side of the front cowl. She is painted in honour of a US colonel, Glen Duncan, whose original nose art had a skeleton with guns and the name *Angel of Death* on the cowling. His superiors were not impressed; hence the change of name. The colonel was credited with 19.5 kills. Originally this aircraft was posted to the Royal Australian Air Force in late 1944, so she is not too far from home.

At Wanaka I saw the first-mentioned Mustang in flight accompanied by a Spitfire, a Corsair, two Kittyhawks, an Avenger, a Yak-3 and the Me-109. Later, the two Mustangs flew together. You really can't better those combinations of World War II fighter aircraft for a major *Wow!* factor.

SPECIFICATIONS

CREW	1
LENGTH	32ft 3in (9.83m)
WINGSPAN	37ft 0in (11.28m)
HEIGHT	13ft 4.5in (4.08m)
WEIGHT EMPTY	7635lb (3465kg)
WEIGHT LOADED	9200lb (4175kg)
POWERPLANT	1 x Packard V-1650-7 V12 engine with intercooled supercharger, 1490hp (1111kW)

PERFORMANCE

MAXIMUM SPEED	437mph (703km/h)
CRUISE SPEED	362mph (580km/h)
RANGE	1650 miles (2755km)
SERVICE CEILING	41,900ft (12,800m)
RATE OF CLIMB	3200ft per min (16.3m per sec)

ARMAMENT

GUNS	6 x 0.50in (12.7mm) AN/M2 Browning machine guns
ROCKETS	6 x 5.0in (127mm) T64 HVAR rockets
BOMBS	1000lb (453kg) total, on 2 wing hardpoints

MITSUBISHI ZERO A6M3

1940

The Japanese Zero was introduced early in the war, mainly as a highly capable aircraft-carrier-based long-range fighter plane. They quickly gained legendary status as one of the best fighters in the world, due to their manoeuvrability and very-long-range airborne capacity. They were also used as a land-based fighter. It was their extreme lightness that helped with their performance and speed, but that came at a cost, with no armour protection for the pilot, and the use of unsealed fuel tanks, which made the Zero prone to turning into a fireball when hit by enemy fire. The Zero could effectively out-turn the best that the Allied forces had to offer. However, by 1943, without any further development, the Zero was becoming outdated. The new American fighters — the Hellcat and the Corsair — soon started to make inroads into the Zero's air supremacy.

The Zero was used extensively in the Pacific theatre, and towards the end of the war they were used in kamikaze (suicide) operations.

The particular Zero featured here, and currently displayed at the Auckland War Memorial Institute and Museum, was captured by the Royal New Zealand Air Force (RNZAF) in September 1945, at Kara Airfield on Bougainville. Her model number is *3844*, and she is a Zero A6M3 model 22. These were the fastest of all the Zero derivatives. This aircraft was built in 1943, and served on an aircraft carrier in the Solomon Islands. She was later adapted for land use and based at Kara Airfield, where she was damaged in an Allied bombing raid in November 1943.

By that stage the Japanese were short of supplies, and there she sat until 1945, when they managed to repair her using some parts off other damaged Zeros. She never flew again before the Kiwis got their hands on her. The RNZAF flew her to Piva Airfield on Bougainville, then shipped her back to Hobsonville Airbase in New Zealand. The Zero was flown one more time in New Zealand before going to Ardmore. From there, she went on display at Ohakea, before being gifted to the Auckland Museum in 1959. She has remained on display ever since.

There is believed to be only 20 Zero fighters left in the world, mostly housed in museums as static displays. One is apparently still flying.

SPECIFICATIONS

CREW	1
LENGTH	29ft 9in (9.06m)
WINGSPAN	39ft 4in (12.0m)
HEIGHT	10ft 0in (3.05m)
WEIGHT EMPTY	3704lb (1680kg)
WEIGHT MAXIMUM	6164lb (2,679kg)
POWERPLANT	1 x Nakajima Sakae radial engine, 1130hp (840kW)

PERFORMANCE

MAXIMUM SPEED	333mph (540km/h)
RANGE	1260 miles (2027km)
WITH DROP TANKS	2030 miles (3267km)
SERVICE CEILING	33,000ft (10,000m)
RATE OF CLIMB	20,000ft (6000m) in 7 min 19 sec

ARMAMENT

GUNS	2 x 7.7mm (.303in) Type 99 machine guns
BOMB LOAD	2 x 132lb (60kg) bombs
	1 x 551lb (250kg) bomb for kamikaze missions

DE HAVILLAND DH.98 MOSQUITO FB Mk.26

1941

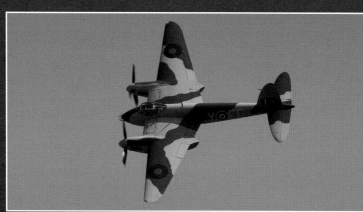

To see what was then the only airworthy Mosquito in the world flying in New Zealand before she departed overseas with her new owner was awe-inspiring, and lots of Kiwis flocked to see her.

As I was writing this book, I was privileged to spend some time with Warren, and was able to photograph not one, but two, more Mosquitos under restoration at his premises. The one that appears more advanced will actually be flying by the time you read this book. Avspecs will finish her while this book is at the printers, so we are truly lucky to be able to show you her in the final stages of her restoration. Again being restored for an overseas buyer, she has a new set of wings and a new Glyn Powell fuselage. The owner bought a 'project Mosquito', so the many thousands of other parts could be restored and used on the restoration. The Mosquito restored in 2012 took out the supreme Grand Champion World War II prize for best restoration at the Oshkosh aircraft show, the first time a British-designed aircraft has done so, and the first time an aircraft restored outside America has won. Accolades to both Avspecs and Glyn Powell. The second restoration is as beautiful as the first, so who knows what accolades will come its way?

Wouldn't it be fantastic to see both of the aircraft flying in formation!

SPECIFICATIONS

CREW	2
LENGTH	41ft 2in (13.57m)
WINGSPAN	54ft 2in (16.52m)
HEIGHT	17ft 5in (5.3m)
WEIGHT EMPTY	13,356lb (6058kg)
WEIGHT LOADED	17,700lb (8028kg)
POWERPLANT	2 x Rolls Royce Merlin 21/21 or 23/23 (left/right) (or Packard Merlin 225) liquid-cooled V12 engines, 1480hp (1103kW) each

PERFORMANCE

MAXIMUM SPEED	366mph (489km/h) Rolls Royce; 380mph (612km/h) Packard
RANGE	900 miles (1400km)
SERVICE CEILING	29,000ft (8839m)
RATE OF CLIMB	1740ft per min (8.8m per sec)

ARMAMENT

GUNS	4 x 20mm (.79in) Hispano cannon (fuselage)
	4 x .303in (7.7mm) Browning machine guns (nose)
BOMBS	2 x 250lb (113kg)

WARREN DENHOLM: THE MAN LEADING AVSPECS

Avspecs Ltd was formed in Rotorua, New Zealand, in 1997 by Warren and Shona Denholm and Colin Denholm. Its purpose was to provide a fully dedicated restoration facility for warbird and vintage aircraft. In 2000, Avspecs moved to Ardmore Airport in South Auckland to be closer to support services. It is now managed by Warren and his wife, Shona. Warren also has a commercial pilot's licence. He started in the aircraft business in the air force's technical area, lasting 13 months and 3 days before leaving and working for a company doing aircraft maintenance, where he gained his qualifications.

Warren's first foray into vintage aircraft happened in 1986, when he moved to Auckland to join the team on the restoration of the Hawker Sea Fury. He maintains that this is where he caught the vintage bug. When Avspecs first opened in 1997, they began repairing the crashed Spitfire of Sir Tim Wallace. Other restorations, besides the Mosquitos, include five P-40 Kittyhawk rebuilds, two Spitfires, a DH89a Rapide, a CAC 31 Sabre, and a CT4 trainer, Tiger Moths and a number of Harvards. Much of their current work is for overseas clients.

On my visit, I spied a past memory being worked on at the back of the workshop. This is an aircraft that Warren and Shona personally own, and she is being quietly beavered away on as and when time allows. To me, she is an iconic aircraft of New Zealand, even though she was designed and flown during the war. It is a Grumman Widgeon flying boat, and boy, does it have a great history …

GRUMMAN G44 WIDGEON AMPHIBIAN

1941

Who among us of experienced years can't remember the larger-than-life Captain Fred Ladd and his famous flying boats of Tourist Air Travel? They operated in Southland and out of Auckland. Many a time, while staying at beaches, I can recall the flying boats dropping in to disembark or pick up passengers, or arriving to give holidaymakers rides. I can remember in 1959 taking off for a ride from Long Bay, Coromandel, with Fred Ladd in his Grumman Widgeon. He was a man of sayings. 'A shower of spray, and we're away' was his takeoff call. And, after Fred, came Sea Bee Air, which operated through to the 1980s, followed by Salt Air in the Bay of Islands in the 1990s. At a later date the Widgeons were sold off and replaced with helicopters. However, Owen Harnish, who was involved with Salt Air, has retained one and is restoring her, as is Warren, who bought another one off Owen.

I thought when I started to write this book that it would be a piece of cake to find one of these aircraft still flying in New Zealand. At the moment, sadly there are none. However, hope is on the horizon. With the efforts of Owen and Warren, maybe one day we will have two of them flying again in New Zealand. The featured plane here is Warren's, and the restoration is quite major. Although the aircraft was all there, after many years of salt-water takeoffs and landings there was deep-seated corrosion throughout the aircraft. This has led to a major rebuild that is still in progress.

So a little history about the Grumman Widgeon is in order, followed by this particular aircraft's history. It is quite fascinating.

The Widgeon was originally designed for civil use, and was designed in 1940 with the first production models arriving in 1941. Production carried on through to 1955. The US Navy became interested in them for use as anti-submarine aircraft, and subsequently used them in the Coast Guard. A total of 276 Widgeons were built by Grumman, with 176 used by the military, both the US Navy and the Royal Navy.

ZK-AVM

Post-war, Grumman re-designed them to make them more useful for civil use. Six seats were installed for passenger work, and a new hull was made for better water-handling. The new version was given the designation 'G44A', and a grand total of 76 were built. Another 41 were built in France under a licence agreement.

At a later date a company in Oregon, by the name of McKinnon Enterprises, converted 70 Widgeons to 'Super Widgeons'. Larger engines were fitted, replacing the originals with 270hp Avco Lycoming flat 6-piston engines. They also fitted an emergency exit, and larger passenger windows, along with more modern avionics.

So what about the New Zealand history, particularly that of Warren's Widgeon? She arrived here in 1950, when Amphibian Airways was formed by an Invercargill businessman. He could see a service catering to the lakes and fiords of the South. This plane, *ZK-AVM*, was imported from Australia and commenced charter work. By 1952, a second Widgeon was added. In 1954, a new company started up, called New Zealand Tourist Air Travel, with Fred Ladd being appointed general manager and chief pilot. He attracted a lot of attention, and by 1960 had added a second Widgeon. In 1962, Tourist Air Travel acquired Amphibian Airways, setting up networks in both the North and South Islands. Further aircraft were added in 1963 and 1964. The year 1967 saw Mount Cook Airline take over Tourist Air Travel, and in 1975 they chose to move away from amphibians. A group of staff, with investor support, then started up Sea Bee Air, doing tourist work around the Hauraki Gulf and Islands. Sea Bee Air closed its amphibian service in 1989, but *ZK-AVM* had already been exported to Australia sometime before this.

In 1992, Grant and Owen Harnish had created Aquatic and Vintage Airways, based in Paihia. Mainly catering for the tourist market, they had started with one Widgeon, then imported *ZK-AVM* back into New Zealand, re-registering her with her old call sign. In 1996, the company changed its name to Salt Air.

ZK-AVM was built in 1946, and was later converted to a 'Super Widgeon'. She was exported to Australia in 1947, owned by a petroleum company who used her in New Guinea. She arrived in New Zealand in December 1950, and remained here, as mentioned above, until 1987, when she again, under an Australian company, flew in Australia before going to New Guinea in 1994. After arriving back in New Zealand, she flew with Salt Air in 1996. The Widgeons were both retired at a later date.

Although progress is slow on *ZK-AVM*, one can see that the work on her continues, and I for one will be absolutely over the moon when she finally takes to the air again. She represents a very special memory for me, and a very special part of New Zealand aviation.

All photographs of the Widgeon are of *ZK-AVM* in her many guises.

SPECIFICATIONS

CREW	1
PASSENGERS	5
LENGTH	31ft 1in (9.47m)
WINGSPAN	40ft 0in (12.19m)
HEIGHT	11ft 5in (3.48m)
WEIGHT EMPTY	3800lb (1724kg)
WEIGHT LOADED	5500lb (2500kg)
POWERPLANT	2 x Continental IO-470 flat sixes engines, 260hp (200kW) each

PERFORMANCE

MAXIMUM SPEED	165 knots (306km/h)
CRUISE SPEED	152 knots (282km/h)
RANGE	920 miles (1481km)
SERVICE CEILING	14,600ft (4450m)
RATE OF CLIMB	700ft per min (3.6m per sec)

GRUMMAN TBF/TBM AVENGER

1942

The Grumman Avenger is an American-designed torpedo bomber. Designated the 'TBF Avenger' by Grumman, they were outsourced to General Motors as a second manufacturer to keep up with the production numbers needed. The General Motors-manufactured aircraft were designated the 'TBM'. Altogether 9836 Avengers were built, with 7546 being built by the aircraft division of General Motors, who took over the majority of the production as Grumman phased down their production so as to increase their output of F6F Hellcat fighters.

During World War II, the Avengers saw action in both the Atlantic and the Pacific theatres of war. A navy aircraft, they were used both off land and from aircraft carriers. Some also saw service with the British Navy and our own Royal New Zealand Air Force (RNZAF).

They carried a crew of three: the pilot; the bombardier/radio operator/ventral gunner; and the turret gunner. They were equipped with two wing-mounted .50-calibre machine guns, a .50-calibre machine gun in the rear turret, and a ventral .30 machine gun. In the bomb bay, they could carry a load of up to 2000lb of bombs or torpedoes or rockets in various combinations. The Avengers were the largest and

heaviest single-engined aircraft in the war. They were also designed with a folding wing to maximise storage room on aircraft carriers. In 1944, General Motors started production on the TBM-3, utilising a more powerful powerplant and wing hardpoints to carry drop tanks and rockets. Over 4000 'Dash 3s' were produced, but most Avengers that saw service in the Pacific were 'Dash 1s'.

In the Pacific they made a name for themselves. In the Battle of Midway, six of the brand-new Avengers were sent out, with five being shot down and the sixth limping home with one dead gunner and a wounded pilot and bombardier/radio operator. However, as the pilots got more experience and developed better operational tactics and attack procedures, their successes started to mount up. In the battle at the Eastern Solomons (August 1942), carrier-based Avengers sank the Japanese light carrier *Ryujo*, and claimed a dive-bomber. Of the 24 aircraft involved, 17 returned. At the naval Battle of Guadalcanal (November 1942), US Marine Corps Avengers from Henderson Airfield and Navy Avengers helped sink the Japanese battleship *Hiei*. This

battle could be heard by servicemen back on Guadalcanal, and at night the gun flashes could be seen. How do I know this? My father was there, having just arrived as one of the forward ground crew for New Zealand 3(GR) Squadron flying Hudson bombers.

Besides hunting and torpedoing surface ships, Avengers also accounted for 30 submarines.

The Avengers in the RNZAF were with 30 and 31 Light Bomber squadrons, and saw active service in the last two years of the war in the Pacific. They operated 48 aircraft, but by the end of the war they were down to 12, the others having gone to the US Navy. Of those 12, 7 were sold for scrap in 1948 and 2 were lost in accidents in 1949 and 1956. Survivors in New Zealand number four. Three New Zealand Avengers are on display: one at the RNZAF Wigram museum, one at the Classic Flyers Museum at Tauranga Airport at Mount Maunganui, which is actually being restored, and one at MOTAT. The fourth is an airworthy example, and is our featured aircraft.

The featured aircraft is a TBM built by General Motors in 1945. She is owned by Brendon Deere, and is based in Ohakea. Brendon saw his first Avenger as a kid in the playground at Havelock North. Having a natural interest in aircraft, he read all about the Avenger, and even made models of them. The Avenger he owns served in a training capacity in San Diego, before post-war moving around a number of US Navy posts, including carrier-based operations. She was sold as navy surplus in 1954, and converted to an insecticide-spraying aircraft and used in forest protection in the United States and Canada. In 1992, she was sold and reconverted back to military configuration for the Old Flying Machine Company in Duxford, England. After two years, she was shipped to New Zealand as part of the Alpine Fighter Collection at Wanaka. In 1998, she was sold to an Australian collector.

Brendon managed to buy her, hired a really good pilot, and as a passenger flew home to New Zealand with her. They flew from Toowoomba to Lord Howell Island, then to Norfolk Island, where they overnighted. From there they flew to Kerikeri. Brendon said it was great to see the top of the North Island, with both crew thinking, 'Great — we are not going to die in a 70-year-old single-engined bomber.' The last leg was to Ohakea. The old girl didn't miss a beat the whole way. They cruised at 10,000 feet across the Tasman. With a little TLC and a full bare-metal repaint, the Avenger was once again ready to fly our skies. This aircraft has had a continuous flying history since 1945, which makes her pretty special. She is now piloted for Brendon by Squadron Leader Jim Rankin, RNZAF (Ohakea). I love watching this old bird fly. She is large for a single-engined aircraft, and certainly has a presence about her.

A couple of notable Americans flew in Avengers during World War II. President George H. Bush (the first President Bush) was one of the youngest Avenger pilots. He earned the Distinguished Flying Cross (DFC) during his airforce career. The other was actor Paul Newman, who was a turret gunner in an Avenger. It was also a group of seven Avengers that mysteriously disappeared in The Bermuda Triangle, never to be seen or heard of again.

SPECIFICATIONS

CREW	3
LENGTH	40ft (12.19m)
WINGSPAN	54ft 2in (16.51m)
HEIGHT	15ft 5in (4.7m)
WEIGHT EMPTY	10,545lb (4783kg)
WEIGHT LOADED	17,893lb (8115kg)
POWERPLANT	1 x Wright R-2600-20 radial engine, 1900hp (1420kW)

PERFORMANCE

MAXIMUM SPEED	275mph (442km/h)
RANGE	1000 miles (1610km)
SERVICE CEILING	30,100ft (9170m)
RATE OF CLIMB	2060ft per min (10.5m per sec)

ARMAMENT

GUNS	2 x .50in (12.7mm) wing-mounted M2 Browning machine guns
	1 x .50in (12.7mm) dorsal-mounted M2 Browning machine gun
	1 x .30in (7.62mm) ventral-mounted M1919 Browning machine gun
	(*Note:* earlier Avengers had a nose-mounted M1919, and no wing-mounted guns)
BOMBS	1 x 2000lb (907kg) Mark 13 torpedo *or* bombs up to 2000lb *or* rockets up to 8 3.5in forward-firing aircraft rockets or high-velocity aerial rockets

MILES M.38 MESSENGER 2A

1942

This little aeroplane really piqued my interest when I first spotted her in the New Zealand Warbirds hangar. I had never seen anything like her, which is not surprising, when you consider that after the 1942 prototype only another 21 were built in 1943, and another 71 post-war. That's a grand total of 93 Miles Messenger aircraft. This little fellow appears to be the only one in New Zealand. She was owned by a private family trust and was just last year given into the care of the New Zealand Warbirds Association.

So what is she all about? A first glance gives you a relatively compact aircraft with a single tractor engine, an enclosed cabin for four, sporting a rather bulbous front windscreen with double-opening hatches for access off the low mono-wings. But it is the tail fin that grabs the attention: she has not got one — she's got three! So I ask again: what is she all about? What is the history behind the design? What is the history of the actual aircraft model?

It really is quite interesting. The Messenger was designed to meet the requirements the British Army had for a robust, slow-speed, low-maintenance air observation post and liaision aircraft. A group of senior army officers initiated the design and prototype, which was built in 1942. It was powered by a de Havilland 140hp Gipsy Moth engine. Obviously from the accompanying photographs, one can see that she was a low-wing monoplane with fixed undercart, but the wing incorporated fixed aerofoil trailing-edge flaps, and the three tail fins were designed for directional stability at very low speeds. Her stall speed was just 25mph. The flight test went very well. An AOP (air observer post) unit tested her, and were highly enthusiastic about her capabilities for her intended role. However, things came to an abrupt halt when the Ministry of Aircraft Production found out about it. They were shocked that this plane had been commissioned, designed and a

prototype built and tested, without them knowing about it, and without their approval. Basically, they got their knickers in a knot and stalked off to sulk for a little bit, before going completely sour and putting the kibosh on the whole project. It didn't matter that the Miles Messenger fitted the intended role perfectly. It was all about certain noses being put out of joint and using political clout to force their point. Bureaucratic nonsense. However, in late 1943, using a clause for a VIP transport role, a small order under the designation 'M.38 Messenger' was slipped through the system, and 21 Miles Messengers were built. The Marshal of the Royal Air Force got one, and Field Marshal Sir Bernard Montgomery got his hands on one, too. The others? History does not really tell us, but let's hope they did what they were intended for.

After the war, the Miles Messenger was built for civilian use. Production ceased in 1948. The post-war aircraft were powered either by the Gipsy Moth engine or the Blackburn Cirrus Major engine.

This particular aircraft is designated as a '2A', and would have been fitted with the Blackburn engine. Only several examples are still flying across the world, so they are now very rare. This New Zealand-registered Messenger has been painted in the correct and original colours of the Messenger that belonged to Field Marshal Montgomery.

SPECIFICATIONS

CREW	1
PASSENGERS	3
LENGTH	24ft 0in (7.32m)
WINGSPAN	36ft 2in (11.03m)
HEIGHT	7ft 6in (2.29m)
WEIGHT EMPTY	1450lb (659kg)
WEIGHT LOADED	2400lb (1091kg)
POWERPLANT	1 x Blackburn Cirrus Major 3 4-cylinder aircooled inline engine, 155hp (116kW)

PERFORMANCE

MAXIMUM SPEED	135mph (219km/h)
RANGE	260 miles (418km)
SERVICE CEILING	16,000ft (4878m)
RATE OF CLIMB	660ft per min (290m per min)

AVRO LANCASTER HEAVY BOMBER

1942

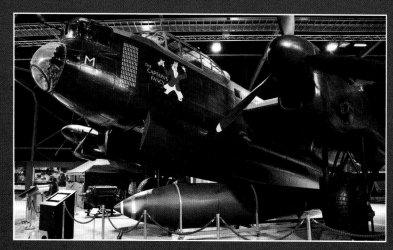

'THE FIGHTERS ARE OUR SALVATION,
BUT THE BOMBERS WILL GIVE US VICTORY'
— Winston Churchill, 1940

The Avro Lancaster was designed in 1940 by Roy Chadwick. He had previously designed the Manchester twin-engined bomber, which was a little unstable and had engines that were prone to overheat and be unreliable. With the Lancaster, he took the Manchester design and lengthened the wingspan 12 feet, and fitted four Rolls Royce Merlin supercharged V12 engines. From the first test-flight in January 1941, they were found to be a beautiful plane to fly, and by 1942 were operational in Bomber Command. The Lancaster went on to become the most famous bomber in World War II. Among their achievements, Lancasters sunk one-third of Germany's U-boat fleet while at anchor in ports. They blew up dams (remember The Dambusters and our own famous and highly decorated pilot, Squadron Leader Sir Leslie Munro?), sank enemy battleships, and bombed factories, dramatically cutting down Germany's ability to produce much-needed aircraft and other military hardware. They also dropped food into Holland and ferried many prisoners of war home after VE Day.

But it wasn't all plain sailing. The attrition rate was incredibly high. Of the 7377 Lancasters built, 3932 were lost in action. The 'Lancs', as they were affectionately known, were, due to the construction and hatches, very hard to exit from in an emergency, and so many of the crews were lost as well. The seven aircrew consisted of the pilot (the skipper), the flight engineer, the navigator, the wireless operator, the bomb-aimer/front-gunner, the mid-gunner, and the tail-gunner. If you were aircrew in a bomber in 1940, you had a 10 per cent chance of being alive by 1945. Not great odds.

Today there are only 23 Lancasters left in the world. A few lie in bits or have partial fuselages on display, a couple lie in situ where they crashed and are protected, two are airworthy, with a third being brought up to airworthy standard, with another able to taxi, and the rest being on static display in museums.

So what is the connection to New Zealand? First, we are very lucky to have a Lancaster here in New Zealand. Our one was built in 1945 and did not see active service in the war. In 1952, she was sold to the French Aeronavale Air Force and served until the 1960s in Vietnam, finishing up in New Caledonia doing search and rescue work around the Pacific. At the end of her service, the French presented the Lancaster to New Zealand as a memorial to the New Zealand airmen who had served in Bomber Command, and in particular in the Lancasters. She flew into Auckland in April 1964, and was donated to the Museum of Transport and Technology (MOTAT) where she has pride of place in their aviation centre. She has been steadily restored under the auspices of the Bomber Command Association (NZ). In doing the restoration, they have configured her to impersonate a rather famous Lancaster from 75 Squadron that was mainly manned by New Zealanders. The 'Lanc' she impersonates flew over 100 missions, and was the squadron's unofficial 'lucky' mascot. She was called *The Captain's Fancy*.

Over 6000 Kiwis served in or were seconded to the Royal Air Force, with over 2000 of them killed in action. They served both in Fighter Command and Bomber Command. There was one Lancaster 75 Squadron and one Fighter 487 Squadron that were mainly manned by New Zealanders, but the majority of New Zealand airmen were not in these squadrons, but flew alongside men from Canada, Australia, South Africa and the United Kingdom. My uncle, Bob Jessen, was a Lancaster bomber pilot serving with 15 Squadron.

SPECIFICATIONS

CREW	7
LENGTH	69ft 4in (21.11m)
WINGSPAN	102ft 0in (31.09m)
HEIGHT	20ft 6in (6.25m)
WEIGHT EMPTY	36,457lb (16,571kg)
WEIGHT MAX. LOADED	68,000lb (30,909kg)
POWERPLANT	4 x Rolls Royce V12 Merlin engines, 1640hp (1223kW) each

PERFORMANCE

MAXIMUM SPEED	287mph (462km/h)
CRUISE SPEED	200mph (321km/h)
RANGE	1550 miles (2495km) maximum payload; 2530 miles (4072km) light payload
SERVICE CEILING	25,000ft (7620m)
RATE OF CLIMB	250ft per min (76m per min)

ARMAMENT

GUNS	8 x 7.7mm Browning machine guns
BOMBS	14,109lb (6400kg)

LANCASTER PILOT PROFILE – PILOT OFFICER G.R. (BOB) JESSEN, RNZAF SECONDED TO RAF

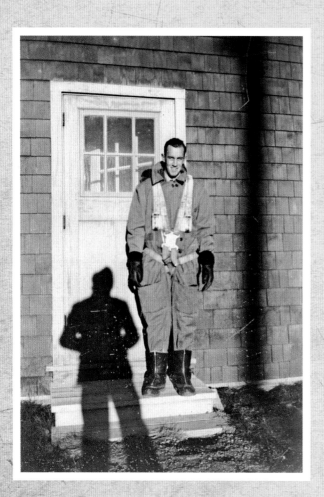

In late 1941, Bob Jessen volunteered for pilot training with the Royal New Zealand Air Force. He was told to go home and wait until they contacted him, as they had too many volunteers and couldn't handle the numbers. Eventually, Bob got sick of waiting and joined the army and was put in the cavalry. Sometime after his basic training and before he went overseas, the air force contacted him, saying could he present himself for pilot training. He was able to transfer to the air force in 1943, and as an LAC (leading aircraftsman) completed his single-engine training as a pilot with a total of 60 hours' flying time. This was done in a Tiger Moth. At this stage he was assessed as good material for flying bombers, and was shipped off to Canada for training on twin-engined aircraft.

According to his logbook, Bob commenced training in Canada on 4 March 1944. The plane he flew was a twin-engined Avro Anson Mk 2 bomber. He completed his training in Canada on 1 April with a total of 220 hours and 5 minutes' flying time. He graduated with

the rank of Flight Sergeant. He embarked by ship to England and began a conversion course in the twin-engined Oxford bomber trainer on 21 September 1944. The advanced training finished on 12 December 1944. It had included navigation, night flying, bombing practice and formation flying.

From here, Bob went on to train on the medium-weight Wellington bomber on 1 February 1945. Over this period the Royal Air Force decided that Bob would make a good Lancaster pilot, so on 5 May he began his conversion, training on Lancasters.

On 8 May, Germany surrendered. Bob's training continued, and on 22 June 1945 he was transferred to 15 Squadron and was promoted to Pilot Officer. He flew 27 missions, to Denmark, Italy and Germany, with his logbook also recording operations with codenames. He flew on food-dropping missions to Holland, and ferried many prisoners of war back to England from Germany and Italy. On his last flight heading to Germany, two engines failed over the Channel, and he nursed his

Lancaster back to England and landed at Woodbridge. His logbook is very understated.

He was repatriated to New Zealand in December 1945, arriving home in 1946. It amazed me how many hours it took to train pilots to fly the Lancaster. There was much more training needed to fly a four-engined Lancaster than to fly a single-engined fighter. A huge investment was made in training, and in the earlier years of the war much of that experience was lost in combat.

There is no doubt that the crews of Lancasters formed a huge bond. Bob and his entire crew stayed in contact until they all passed away in their old age.

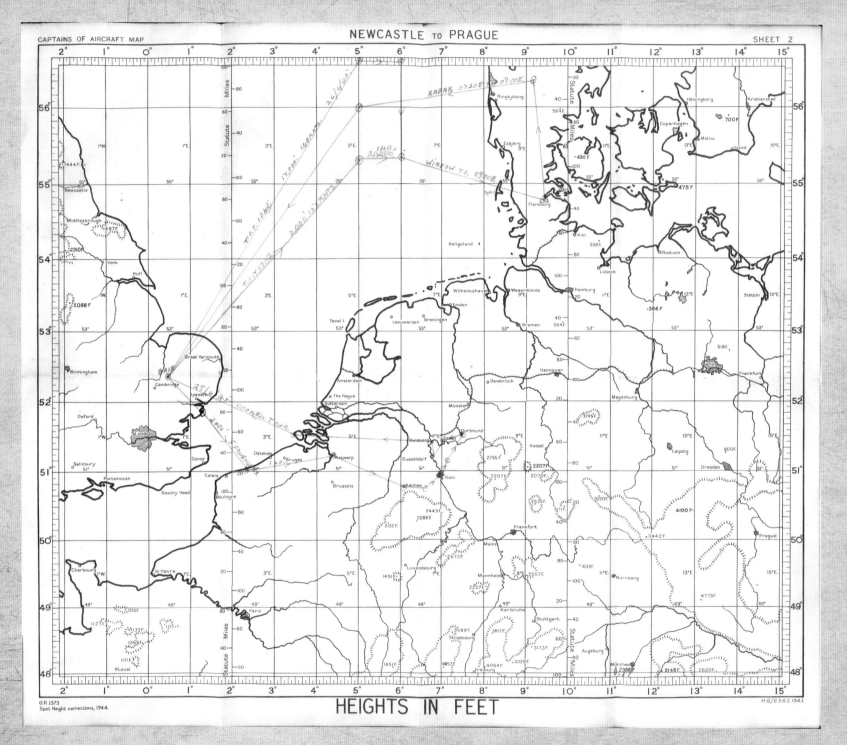

HEIGHTS IN FEET

O.R.1373
Spot Height corrections, 1944.

H.Q./G.S.G.S. 1943

KEY TO *Fig. 1*

INSTRUMENT PANEL

1. Instrument flying panel.
2. D.F. Indicator.
3. Landing light switches.
4. Undercarriage indicator switch.
5. D.R. compass repeater.
6. D. R. compass deviation card holder.
7. Ignition switches.
8. Boost gauges.
9. R.p.m. indicators.
10. Booster coil switch.
11. Slow-running cut-out switches.
12. I.F.F. detonator buttons.
13. I.F.F. switch.
14. Engine starter switches.
15. Bomb containers jettison button.
16. Bomb jettison control.
17. Vacuum change-over cock.
18. Oxygen regulator.
19. Feathering buttons.
20. Triple pressure gauge.
21. Signalling switchbox (identification lamps).
22. Fire-extinguisher pushbuttons.
23. Suction gauge.
24. Starboard master engine cocks.
25. Supercharger gear change control panel.
26. Flaps position indicator.
27. Flaps position indicator switch.
28. Throttle levers.
29. Propeller speed control levers.
30. Port master engine cocks.
31. Rudder pedal.
32. Boost control cut-out.
33. Signalling switchbox (recognition lights).
34. Identification lights colour selector switches.
35. D.R. compass switches.
36. Auto controls steering lever.
37. P.4 compass deviation card holder.
38. P.4 compass.
39. Undercarriage position indicator.
40. A.S.I. correction card hold.
41. Beam approach indicator.
42. Watch holder.

INSTRUMENT PANEL.

FIG 1   FIG 1

YAKOVLEV YAK-3

1944

It wasn't until late in the writing of this book that I came across the Yak-3. The aircraft was in the Warbirds Park at Wanaka. She was obviously Russian — I knew that from the paint job. To me, she had similarities to the Spitfire. A Russian Spitfire? Yeah, nah! As a Warbirds pilot wandered past me, I asked him, 'What is this aircraft?' The reply was a Yak-3. Now, I was familiar with the Yak-52, but this was definitely something new. I hauled out my programme and there she was.

The Yak-3s had been a Russian-produced fighter from 1944, sporting a V12 engine. They were light, highly manoeuvrable and highly effective, particularly against the Messerschmitt Bf 109. By mid-1946, over 4800 had been built. They were a forgiving, easy-to-handle aircraft loved by both novice and experienced pilots alike.

None of the original Yak-3s had survived in an airworthy state, and those that had survived were too far-gone to be brought back to airworthiness. However, in the early 1990s the Yakovlev Design Bureau unearthed the original plans of the Yak-3, including the original jigs and dies. Given the fact that none of these iconic aircraft of the Great Patriotic War had survived, they decided to manufacture 10 new-build Yak-3s. These are a true replica built on the original jigs. As the old Klimov V12 engines were no longer in existence, the new-builds were powered with an Allison V-1710 engine. They are designated as a Yakovlev Yak-3M.

The new aircraft performs as well as the originals did, and is an awesome World War II replica fighter. Several now reside in the United States, some in Australia, and of course that is what we have here in Wanaka. This particular aircraft (serial number 0470106) was first sold to Reno race pilot Tiger Destefani in 1996, before being on-sold. She later crashed on takeoff at Reno in 1999.

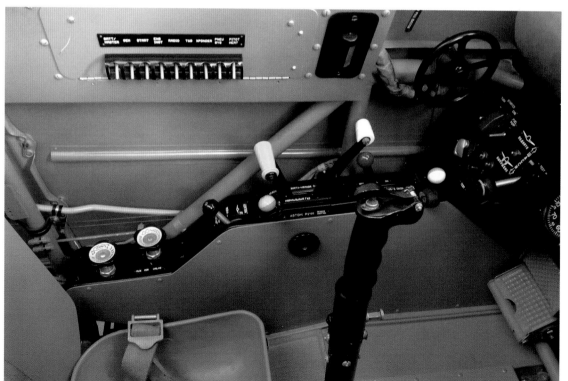

New Zealander Graeme Frew purchased the Yak-3 in 2004, and Jay McIntyre's JEM Aviation did a restoration over a four-year period. While this was taking place, they built in a second seat under the same canopy, and the engine was sent to America for an overhaul. The Yak is painted in the colours of Major Baranov of the 4 Guards Regiment of the Soviet Air Force. The Yak, when not in use, is on display at the Omaka Aviation Heritage Centre in Blenheim. She is positioned in a Russian wartime diorama.

Graeme also gives joyrides under the name Fighter Flights, where one can experience the thrill of flying in one of the fastest wartime fighter planes.

We saw the aircraft in flight, and she was a joy to watch. She looked totally right when flying in the company of other World War II fighters. In one flypast I saw and counted two Kittyhawks, a Corsair, a Spitfire, a Mustang, a Messerschmitt Bf 109 and of course the Yak-3M. The group looked just outstanding.

SPECIFICATIONS

CREW	1
LENGTH	27ft 10in (8.5m)
WINGSPAN	30ft 2in (9.2m)
HEIGHT	7ft 11in (2.39m)
WEIGHT EMPTY	4640lb (2105kg)
WEIGHT LOADED	5864lb (2692kg)
POWERPLANT (ORIGINAL)	1 x Klimov VK-105PF-2 V12 liquid-cooled piston engine, 1300hp (970kW)
POWERPLANT (REPLICA)	1 x Allison V-1710 V12 engine, 1150hp (858kW)

PERFORMANCE

MAXIMUM SPEED	407mph (655km/h)
RANGE	405 miles (650km)
SERVICE CEILING	35,000ft (10,700m)
RATE OF CLIMB	3645ft per min (18.5m per sec)

ARMAMENT

GUNS	1 x 20mm ShVAK cannon
	2 x 12.7mm Berezin UBS machine guns

DE HAVILLAND VAMPIRE JET

1945

The De Havilland DH.100 Vampire was a British jet fighter that entered service with the Royal Air Force (RAF) in 1945. The prototype flew in 1943, but production models arrived too late to be used in combat in World War II. They were Britain's second jet fighter, after the Gloster Meteor, but their first single-engined jet fighter. They were used as a frontline fighter by the RAF until 1951. Just under 3300 Vampires were manufactured, and served in air forces all over the world, including New Zealand.

14 Squadron (Royal New Zealand Air Force) was equipped with 16 Vampire jets in 1952. The squadron was attached to the RAF's Middle East air force, and was based in Cyprus from 1952 until 1955. In 1955, the Vampires of 14 Squadron were replaced with their successor, the De Havilland Venom jet fighter. 75 Squadron also flew Vampires. Most of the Vampires went into storage around 1957/58.

Some static versions remain in New Zealand museums and elsewhere. One is a guardian-post aircraft at the entry to Ohakea air force base. In more recent times, two airworthy versions were imported to New Zealand. One, a DH.100, was imported in 1990 from Australia, and resides in Christchurch.

This Vampire is owned by John Currie. The other, a DH.115, was imported in 1995 by Brett Emeny, and resides in New Plymouth. I was able to get up close and personal with this second Vampire, and had the opportunity to talk to Brett about this plane and some other classics in his hangar. She is ex-Swiss Air Force. After her discharge, she was privately owned. In 1986, she was completely overhauled, and she had flown only 90 hours on the rebuild when Brett bought her. She was brought to New Zealand and painted up in 75 Squadron colours. The highest-numbered Vampire in the squadron was 5711, so Brett put the number 5712 onto his Vampire. She is still regularly flown by Brett, and is often seen at the three New Zealand airshows.

In 2016, both Vampires were seen in the air together, flying in tight formation, and not only together but also in tight box formation with two Strikemasters (see page 326). These old jets are simply incredible, and to think that in just 30-odd years the world went from the fabric, wire and wooden-propeller-driven aircraft of World War I to these amazing jet fighters. It just shows how quickly aircraft technology developed.

SPECIFICATIONS

CREW	1
LENGTH	30ft 9in (9.37m)
WINGSPAN	38ft 9in (11.58m)
HEIGHT	8ft 10in (11.58m)
WEIGHT EMPTY	7283lb (3304kg)
WEIGHT LOADED	12,390lb (5620kg)
POWERPLANT	1 x de Havilland Goblin 3 centrifugal turbojet engine, 3350lbf (14.90 kN)

PERFORMANCE

MAXIMUM SPEED	548mph (882km/h)
RANGE	1220 miles (1960km)
SERVICE CEILING	42,800ft (13,045m)
RATE OF CLIMB	4800ft per min (24.4m per sec)

ARMAMENT

GUNS	4 x 0.79in (20mm) Hispano MKV cannon
ROCKETS	8 x 3in '60lb' rockets
BOMBS	2 x 500lb (225kg) bombs, or 2 drop fuel tanks

POST-WAR AIRCRAFT

Following World War II, aviation came of age in New Zealand. By the last year of the war, jet fighters were already being used, so technology had taken a great leap forward in aviation terms. In New Zealand, we saw the birth of air travel (both domestically and overseas), we saw the entrance of air-freight companies, and of course we saw the beginning of our own topdressing (cropdusting) industry. Other companies started up small air tourism operations, and the use of light aircraft, mainly with aero clubs, began to emerge.

In this section we feature some of the iconic aircraft, both civil and military, that have been well-known over the post-war years, and that have flown — and, in some cases, still do fly — our skies. We have also been privileged to be able to feature the RNZAF Hercules and Orion aircraft that have served our country so well over the years. These aircraft have stood the test of time, and have served, and continue to serve, in many air forces across the world.

AUSTER J-1

1945

The Auster was first produced in 1945 and went through to 1952. It became one of Britain's most successful post-war light aircraft, with over 400 built. Many were converted, like our featured aircraft, to the J-1B configuration, with the larger tail fin and the 130hp Gypsy Major engine. Starting in 1946, Austers were exported directly from the factory to many countries, including Argentina, Australia, Belgium, Brazil, Ceylon, Denmark, Egypt, France, Iraq, Jordan, the Netherlands, New Zealand, Norway, Pakistan, South Africa, Southern Rhodesia, Sweden, Switzerland, Trinidad and Tobago, Uganda and Uruguay. Not too bad an effort on the part of the manufacturers.

ZK-AOB (Alpha, Oscar, Bravo) was imported into New Zealand as a brand-new aircraft and registered on 19 February 1947. Brought in by agents Boon and Co Ltd, she was sold to a Mr Eric Grey of Hokianga in June of that year. This aircraft was to go through the hands of a long succession of well-known aviation personalities. One of the owners, Faranty Desborough, converted her to a J-1B with a Gypsy Major engine and a larger tail fin and rudder. In 1962, she went to owner Brian Hore, after which she passed through another nine owners. Her registration was cancelled in 1991, but renewed when previous owner Brian Hore of Nokomai Station re-acquired and restored her in 2001. He has been flying her regularly since then. We recently watched him in a STOL (short takeoff and landing) competition, where he was up against much more modern aircraft that had been specifically designed for these competitions. He was incredibly consistent and took out third place, which I think was pretty darn good with a 1947 aircraft.

Sometimes, when this aircraft is resting, she takes time out at the Croydon Aviation Heritage Centre, and it was here that we first came across the little Auster. Brian has made a beautiful job of the restoration, and the aircraft is pristine, as can be seen in the photographs.

SPECIFICATIONS

CREW	1
PASSENGERS	2
LENGTH	23ft 5in (7.1m)
WINGSPAN	36ft 0in (10.97m)
HEIGHT	6ft 6in (1.98m)
WEIGHT EMPTY	1052lb (478kg)
WEIGHT LOADED	1850lb (841kg)
POWERPLANT	1 x Blackburn Cirrus Minor 2 engine, 100hp (76kW)

PERFORMANCE

MAXIMUM SPEED	120mph (194km/h)
RANGE	320 miles (515km)
SERVICE CEILING	14,000ft (4300m)

With the J-1B conversion, the weight increased and the horsepower increased, changing the specs to:

WEIGHT EMPTY	1223lb (555kg)
WEIGHT LOADED	2000lb (907kg)
POWERPLANT	1 x de Havilland Gypsy Major engine, 130hp (97kW)
MAXIMUM SPEED	126mph (203km/h)

SHORT SOLENT S45A Mk IV FLYING BOAT

1946

The Solent Mk IV flying boat featured here was purchased in December 1949, along with three other Mk IV Solents, by our international airline, TEAL. 'TEAL' stood for 'Tasman Empire Airways Ltd', and its shareholding was made up of the New Zealand government, Union Airways, Imperial Airways and Qantas. TEAL was formed in the 1930s, and operated trans-Tasman flights from 1940 through to 1949, using both Solent Mk IIIs and Sandringham flying boats.

The Solent MK IVs were an upgrade, and not only flew trans-Tasman, but also introduced the Coral Route, which covered the Pacific Islands. Flying times for the Coral Route were as follows: Auckland (7.30 hours)—Fiji (3.45 hours)—Samoa (5 hours)—Cook Islands (4 hours)—Tahiti. The trans-Tasman flight time was around seven hours.

The Solents were manufactured in Ireland and were known as the 'Short Solent', Short being part of the manufacturing company's name. It was a progression of the Short Sealord flying boat, which in turn was a progression of the famous Short Sunderland flying boats that were used by New Zealand during World War II. The four New Zealand Solents were the last Solents produced by the Short Company.

In March 1954, TEAL started to acquire land-based aircraft, which began to replace the routes flown by the flying boats. Some of the Solents were consequently sold off. The last Solent commercial flight was on 15 September 1960, from Fiji to Auckland. It was this very plane featured here that made the flight. The registration of this plane was *ZK-AMO* and her name is *Aranui*. After the flight, which landed in Mechanics Bay, she was towed to Hobsonville and put into storage. At a later date she was handed over to MOTAT, who had no option at the time other than to display her outside.

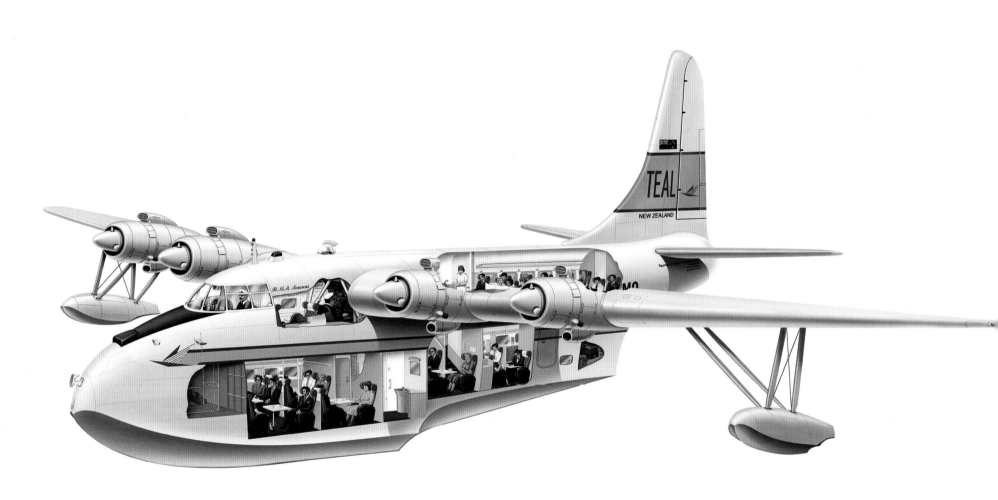

Over the years her condition deteriorated, and with the advent of the giant hangar she was moved inside. Presently, *Aranui* is undergoing an interior restoration, with some areas finished and others underway.

The first impression of the Solent is one of massive size. This plane is huge, and dominates all of the other planes in the massive hangar. She is so tall that part of the tail fin has had to be removed to be able to fit her in the hangar. The tail section sits alongside the aircraft. To a boatie like myself, I found the 'hull' shape very interesting. Designed for (in boating terms) high-speed takeoffs, it had to be able to break from the

sea and lift a fully laden load of some 36,740-odd kilograms into the air. The engineering involved is simply fantastic.

Inside, one is transported back to a bygone era of yesteryear. (See the poster cutaway and the photographs of the interior.) Flying overseas in one of these must have been a real adventure, and quite luxurious if you had the use of one of the lower-deck cabins.

SPECIFICATIONS

CREW	8 (captain, first officer, navigator, radio operator, flight engineer, 2 stewards, 1 stewardess; on occasions, an airline clerk would accompany the crew to help passengers with their official papers)
PASSENGERS	45
LENGTH	89ft 8in (27.4m)
WING SPAN	112ft (34.5m)
LENGTH	89.8ft (27.4m)
HEIGHT	37.3ft (11.4m)
WEIGHT DRY	48,008lb (22,217kg)
WEIGHT MAXIMUM	81,000lb (36,742kg)
POWERPLANT	4 x Bristol Hercules 733 engines, 2040hp (1521kW) each

PERFORMANCE

MAXIMUM SPEED	276mph (444km/h)
CRUISE SPEED	244mph (393km/h)
RANGE	2330 miles (3745km)
SERVICE CEILING	17,000ft (5180m)
RATE OF CLIMB	925ft per min (4.7m per sec)

BRISTOL FREIGHTER 170

1946

A book on New Zealand aviation would not be complete without the iconic old Bristol freighter. The Bristol freighter was designed in 1945, with a prototype flying in 1946. The third build was the first Bristol freighter to have the double opening doors up front. The first commercial aircraft was flying in 1948. Probably best known in New Zealand for their service with SAFE Air and the Royal New Zealand Air Force (RNZAF), these old birds started flying here in 1951. From that period through to around 1986, the Bristol freighters were seen flying in and out of airports all around New Zealand. At one time SAFE Air had 13 in their fleet. 'SAFE' stood for 'Straits Air Freight Express'. The company was based in Blenheim. Today a lone SAFE Air Bristol Freighter resides at Blenheim Airport. She can be taxied, but is not airworthy.

The RNZAF also flew Bristol freighters. They ordered 12 aircraft, with the first arriving in 1951, and by 1955 41 Squadron had four of them. The others were spread across 3 Squadron and 1 Squadron. The Bristol freighters were deployed to Singapore, Malaya, Borneo and Thailand between the mid-1950s and the early 1960s. In the late 1960s and the early 1970s, they were involved flying weekly supply services to South Vietnam for our military personnel stationed there. The Bristol freighters were replaced by Andovers in 1977.

Today, a complete but static RNZAF Bristol freighter is displayed at the Air Force Museum of New Zealand at Wigram, in Christchurch.

SPECIFICATIONS

CREW	2
LENGTH	73ft 4in (22.4m)
WINGSPAN	108ft 0in (32.9m)
HEIGHT	25ft 0in (7.62m)
WEIGHT EMPTY	29,950lb (13,404kg)
WEIGHT LOADED	44,000lb (19,958kg)
POWERPLANT	2 x Bristol Hercules 734 14-cylinder sleeve-valve radial piston engines, 1980hp (1476kW) each

PERFORMANCE

MAXIMUM SPEED	225mph (362km/h)
RANGE	820 miles (1320km)
SERVICE CEILING	24,000ft (7470m)
RATE OF CLIMB	650ft per min (3.3m per sec)

crashed in whiteout conditions and was written-off in 1960. They were also used around the world for aerial topdressing (cropdusting). Overall, 1657 were built.

We have three of the flying examples in New Zealand featured in this book.

Our first featured Beaver is a Warbird registered as *ZK-CKH*, which was the first Beaver to be exported to South Africa, in 1948. She then went to England in 1951. From there, she flew in Libya and in several other North African countries, where she was supposedly running guns, before she was imported into New Zealand in 1965. Here, she was used for agricultural work through to the mid-1980s, when a downturn in topdressing put her back on the market.

Domiciled in Gisborne, she was purchased by an Ardmore-based Warbirds syndicate and restored. She can be seen regularly around Auckland, and often makes flights into Whitianga, which is where I first came across her. She is an immaculate old girl, and I often watch her fly over our Whitianga beach home. She is a land-based Beaver, with two landing wheels and a tail wheel.

The second is an amphibian Beaver. She has both floats and wheels, so obviously can take off and touch down on either land or water. This Beaver is one of two owned by Auckland Seaplanes, a charter and sightseeing company operating off the Auckland Harbour. Her registration is *ZK-WKA* (Waka, Maori for 'canoe' or 'vessel'). She is beautifully presented, and it is a grand sight watching her take off and land on the harbour. It brings back memories of Fred Ladd and his Tourist Air Travel in his Grumman Widgeon flying boats. This particular Beaver was built in 1965, serial number 1585. She was sold directly to the Kenyan Air Force as a wheeled Beaver. Her duties included reconnaissance, along with the role of a bomber! Upon retirement from the Kenyan Air Force, she was purchased by an American, formerly a fighter pilot and at the time an airline pilot. It was his toy, and he amphibianised her and stored her in Canada, some 200 kilometres north of Toronto at the Muskoka Lakes. He owned her for 22 years. When the owner of Auckland Seaplanes, Chris Sattler, purchased the Beaver, she had 8200 hours on the airframe,

and, having been used on fresh-water lakes, showed no signs of corrosion or deterioration. It was obvious that a lot of care had been lavished on the aircraft.

The third of the Beavers is also owned by Auckland Seaplanes, and is a straight seaplane conversion. She is water-based only, and cannot touch down on land. This one was manufactured in 1961, serial number 1477. When manufactured, she sported wheels, and was purchased by the Ghana Air Force. She was limited to around 100 hours' flying time per year, as the air force wasn't over-endowed with capital. She was on-sold in 1973, with a total of 1200 hours on the airframe. She was bought by Air Whitsunday and converted to a seaplane. The Beaver was with them for 15 years, before going to Vancouver, Canada, and into private ownership. She was used to fly out to a private fishing lodge, and was the owner's toy. He owned her for 23 years, before reluctantly letting her go, as he had got too old to hold his private pilot's licence. Chris actually purchased this Beaver before the amphibian, and she has reportedly the lowest airframe hours of any Beaver in the world.

The owner of Auckland Seaplanes, Chris Sattler, is German by birth, and served in the German Air Force as an engineer in the technical wing. It was there that he gained his private pilot's licence, and later on his commercial licence. After living in different parts of the world, he ended up in Auckland, buying a house that overlooked the harbour. It was here that he realised the potential for seaplanes, but couldn't understand why there weren't any flying. A little research showed that Sea Bee Air had changed to helicopters when the high-speed ferries had started up in the harbour in the 1980s and their float-plane services had gone into serious decline. Chris went and worked for a seaplane outfit in Sydney for two years, to learn how to operate such a company, and in the meantime started negotiations to declare an airfield on the Waitemata Harbour. After 'jumping through many hoops', he accomplished the task with the area from the Hilton Hotel across to Stanley Point and up to the harbour bridge designated as an official harbour airport.

When it came to aeroplanes, the Beaver became the obvious choice, with her carrying capacity, her short landing and takeoff abilities, and her powerful engine. She has proved to be a wise choice, and a flight in these Beavers is highly recommended — according to the American, English and German tourists I talked to on the day of my interview with Chris. What better recommendation can you have?

SPECIFICATIONS

CREW	1
PASSENGERS	6
LENGTH	30ft 3in (9.22m)
WINGSPAN	48ft 0in (14.63m)
HEIGHT	9ft 0in (2.74m)
WEIGHT EMPTY	3000lb (1361kg)
WEIGHT LOADED	5100lb (2313kg)
POWERPLANT	1 x Pratt & Whitney R-985 Wasp Junior radial engine, 450hp (336kW)

PERFORMANCE

MAXIMUM SPEED	158mph (255km/h)
CRUISE SPEED	143mph (230km/h)
RANGE	455 miles (732km)
SERVICE CEILING	18,000ft (5486m)
RATE OF CLIMB	1020ft per min (5.2m per sec)

DE HAVILLAND DH 112 VENOM

1949

The Venom was a post-war jet fighter developed from the Vampire. She served with the Royal Air Force as a single-seat fighter-bomber and a two-seat night-fighter. In 1948, de Havilland suggested a development of the Vampire, incorporating a thinner wing and a more powerful engine as a high-altitude fighter. Sharing the same twin-boom tail and the same composite wood/metal structure as the Vampire, but with subtle differences, the Venom was fitted with the new, more powerful de Havilland Ghost engine, as opposed to the Vampire's de Havilland Goblin jet engine. A prototype first flew in 1949. The first variant entered service in 1952, and was the single-seat FB1 fighter-bomber. In 1950, a second prototype variant flew for the first time. She was a night-fighter version, and, to accommodate a two-man crew, she needed some structural modifications, with the crew sitting side by side. She was designated the 'NF2', and entered service in 1955.

Venoms were lent to the Royal New Zealand Air Force, and saw service in the Malayan conflict between 1955 and 1958. They were much faster than the Vampires, with a top speed of 600mph and an ability to outclimb many later jets, including the Strikemaster and the Skyhawk. The late Trevor Bland, founder and past president of the New Zealand Warbirds Association, flew a Venom in the Malayan conflict. The Venom also saw service with the Swiss Air Force, and finally retired in 1983.

Pilot and businessman John Luff purchased a Venom from the Biel family, who had imported her in 1992 from Switzerland, but before he could even learn to fly her, the Venom was written-off in an accident at Masterton. Fortunately, the pilot was incredibly lucky and walked away from the wreck.

John heard about a second Venom for sale in a Swiss museum at Altenrhein, and so sent his friend and old-time aircraft engineer, Gerry Gaston, who had worked on his first Venom, across to Switzerland to check her out. Gerry reported that she was a good one. By this time John had completed several hours' flying time in a dual-control Vampire, so he flew to Switzerland to buy the Venom. While there, he racked up more flying time in the Vampires. The Venom was crated up in 2012, but a drought had affected the river levels in the river Rhine, and ships could not get out, so she sat in a container for a month before moving. At this time, a few unexploded World War II bombs were found in the Rhine, as they had become uncovered with the low water level.

John's Venom is the third airworthy Venom to come to New Zealand.

The first was owned by Trevor Bland, and flew for the first time in 1987. Unfortunately, she suffered engine failure on takeoff and crashed, and was written-off in 1991. Fortunately, once again the pilot walked away. All three Venoms have had the call sign *ZK-VNM*. John has painted his Venom up in the RNZAF colours of Trevor's old 14 Squadron, and she has the personal markings of Trevor's actual RNZAF Venom painted on her.

When she was reassembled, she was test-flown by Squadron Leader Sean Perrett from Ohakea. John completed some more training hours in an L39 jet trainer with Squadron Leader Jim Rankin, before making the jump to the Venom. He has now clocked up 30 hours flying the Venom. Marilyn and I were fortunate enough to spend some time with John, and also to watch him fly the Venom in a beautiful display at Tauranga.

SPECIFICATIONS

CREW	1
LENGTH	31ft 10in (9.70m)
WINGSPAN	41ft 8in (12.70m)
HEIGHT	6ft 2in (1.88m)
WEIGHT EMPTY	9202lb (4173 kg)
WEIGHT LOADED	15,400lb (7000kg)
POWERPLANT	1 x de Havilland Ghost 103 turbojet engine, 4850lbf (21.6kN)

PERFORMANCE

MAXIMUM SPEED	640mph (1030km/h)
RANGE	1080 miles (1730km)
SERVICE CEILING	39,400ft (12,000m)
RATE OF CLIMB	9000ft per min (45.7m per sec)

ARMAMENT

GUNS	4 x .79in (20mm) Hispano Mk.V cannon
ROCKETS	8 x RP-3 60lb (27kg) rockets *or*
BOMBS	2 x 1000lb (454kg) MC bombs

DE HAVILLAND CHIPMUNK DHC-1

1952

I first came across the Chipmunk at a Warbirds open day at Ardmore. There, I learned that they had been designed in 1946 as a replacement trainer for the Royal Canadian Air Force (RCAF) and the Royal Air Force (RAF). The trainer they were superseding was the venerable and legendary Tiger Moth. Using a tuned version of the de Havilland Gipsy Major engine, which developed 145hp, the Chipmunk out-performed the Tiger Moth in all respects. A single-wing plane, they were built with a light aluminium-skinned fuselage, with the fore part or leading edge of the wing formed with aluminium spars and covered in an aluminium skin. The aft part of the wing and the flaps were fabric-covered. Being a two-seater, the pilot and student/passenger sat in tandem in dual-control cockpits, connected by headphones and a mike. The two air forces used the Chipmunk for some years, often as Air Training Corps trainers with universities. From the mid-1960s on, the RAF and RCAF slowly started selling some off and whittling down their numbers. Known as such a well-mannered aircraft, but still having some character, they were quickly bought up by civilian pilots and syndicates.

A week or two after having put the Chipmunk on my list of aircraft to feature, I was getting some paintwork done on our house. With the house being a very tall multi-level home on a sloped section, scaffolding was just not going to work, so I was using a local abseiling company. I got into conversation with one of the lads and, when I mentioned this book, he said, 'You need to talk to my boss. He has a 1952 Chipmunk at a private field here in town.' So on 29 January 2016, Marilyn and I met Neil at the aerodrome, where he showed us his 1952 Chipmunk. She is an original specimen in every respect. Apparently, the original Chipmunks are quite rare now, with a lot of existing ones across the globe having been repowered with different engine options, some having had new instruments fitted, and others having been strengthened for more active aerobatic work.

Neil has the complete history of this aircraft. She was built in England, her constructor's number being *C1-0633*, and was commissioned around 30 April 1952, straight into the RAF. She was decommissioned in 1966, becoming non-effective stock, then in 1975 was sold to the Wycombe Gliding School Syndicate. At this point in time the airframe hours were 6942, and the engine hours 258. She was one of nine Chipmunks offered under a Ministry of Defence sale. In late 1994, she was exported to New Zealand in the hands of DH Chipmunk Syndicate, and registered as *ZK-UAS*. Neil and a partner bought her in early 2012.

Neil holds a private pilot's licence, and has around 400 hours' flying time. He absolutely loves flying the Chipmunk, and very quickly offered Marilyn and myself a ride. It is some time since we both flew in a small aircraft — like at least 15 years ago — and it is 40 years since I had accumulated my 49 hours in a Cherokee 140. So naturally we were both quite excited by the prospect. I was first up, and Neil gave me a briefing and got me strapped into the rear cockpit. We flew out to the west coast, Raglan way, where we executed a couple of steep turns, my first in 40 years. Neil then got me to shadow him on the controls. We came back to the strip and did a sideslip to lose some height, then did a touch-and-go, to give Marilyn some ground-to-air photo opportunities. Coming back in, Neil executed a perfect three-point landing.

After that it was Marilyn's turn, and she came back absolutely buzzing. I shouldn't have been surprised — she has always loved flying in small planes. It made us realise how easy it is to get trapped into everyday life and not take time out to have fun. And that is Neil's philosophy. He says, 'I love flying, and if I am going to fly, it should be in an aircraft that is fun to fly, and this Chipmunk fits the bill perfectly.'

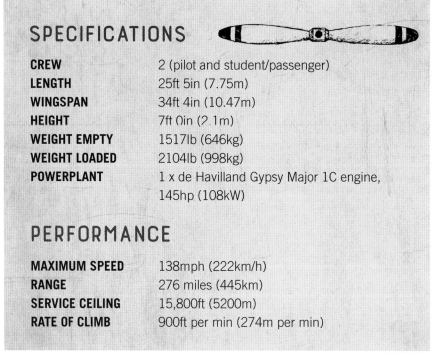

SPECIFICATIONS

CREW	2 (pilot and student/passenger)
LENGTH	25ft 5in (7.75m)
WINGSPAN	34ft 4in (10.47m)
HEIGHT	7ft 0in (2.1m)
WEIGHT EMPTY	1517lb (646kg)
WEIGHT LOADED	2104lb (998kg)
POWERPLANT	1 x de Havilland Gypsy Major 1C engine, 145hp (108kW)

PERFORMANCE

MAXIMUM SPEED	138mph (222km/h)
RANGE	276 miles (445km)
SERVICE CEILING	15,800ft (5200m)
RATE OF CLIMB	900ft per min (274m per min)

SKYHAWK JET

1954

The Skyhawk achieved almost legendary status in New Zealand during their airforce years as our strike force. They certainly were an iconic aircraft in our fair country. With the prototype flying in 1954, the Skyhawk reached production status in 1956. They were built by the McDonnell Douglas Corporation. A lightweight fighter-bomber, the aircraft went through many developments, resulting in more than 15 models or variants of the same plane, including both two-seat and single-seat models. Nearly 2960 aircraft were built by the time production ended in 1979, and they served in air forces all over the world.

The Royal New Zealand Air Force (RNZAF) received its first batch of Skyhawks in 1970, and the aircraft were finally retired in 2001. The initial batch consisted of 14 aircraft: 10 'A-4K' variants and four 'TA-4K' variants. They were allocated to 75 Squadron. The second batch of Skyhawks were eight ex-Royal Australian Navy aircraft. These were bought in 1984, and were assigned to 2 Squadron. Of the Aussie batch, four had been new-build 1967 'A-4G' models for the Australians, and four were 'TA-4G' models. The latter four had been US Navy A-4Fs which had been modified to 'G' specs in 1971, before going to the Aussies. They were also 1967 new-builds. From 1988 through to 1991, the Skyhawks went through a major upgrade programme, which included installing glass cockpits, heads-up display, new acquisition/tracking radars and navigational equipment, wing resparring, and landing gear upgrades. The Skyhawks were used in Australia, Fiji, Hawaii, Singapore and Malaysia on exercises, with the balance of their time in New Zealand.

FLT LT A.R. KEITH

01

CLASSIC FLYERS

The first A4K built by McDonnell Douglas for the RNZAF in 1969 and, together with the TA4K 6251, first to be ceremonially handed over to RNZAF on 16 January 1970.

First flew 10 November 1969; last flew 17 December 2001 after 32 years service and 7568 total flight hours.

RNZAF

A4K SKYHAWK

With a change of government, the Skyhawks were not only retired but were disbanded to be sold off. The fighter wing was effectively abolished. At the time there was a heck of a hue and cry, but the government's decision prevailed. However, the proposed sale fell over, and the Skyhawks were mothballed, except for three, which were retained as demonstrators for potential buyers. Eventually, eight were sold off to a company in the United States, with another nine going to museums around the country. You can see these Skyhawks dotted through MOTAT and Ardmore (Auckland), Classic Flyers (Mount Maunganui), Omaka Aviation Heritage Centre (Blenheim), Wigram (Christchurch), and Ashburton and Wanaka museums.

They are a grand-looking aircraft and, although they are all in static display, they are no less impressive than they were in their heyday. You can get almost into the cockpit in some of the displays. I have to admit, though, that I do miss the display flying that the RNZAF used to do. I would love to see a couple of them flying again!

SPECIFICATIONS

CREW	1 (2 in some models)
LENGTH	40ft 3in (12.22m)
WINGSPAN	26ft 6in (8.38m)
HEIGHT	15ft 0in (4.57m)
WEIGHT EMPTY	10,450lb (4750kg)
WEIGHT LOADED	18,300lb (8318kg)
POWERPLANT	1 x Pratt & Whitney J52-P8A turbojet engine, 9300lbf (41kN)

PERFORMANCE

MAXIMUM SPEED	673mph (1083km/h)
RANGE	2000 miles (3220km)
SERVICE CEILING	42,250ft (12,880m)
RATE OF CLIMB	8440ft per min (43m per sec)

ARMAMENT

GUNS	2 x 20mm (0.79in) Colt Mk 12 cannon
ROCKETS	4 x LAU-10 rocket pods (each with 4 x 127mm Mk32 Zuni rockets)
MISSILES	
air-to-air	4 x AIM-9 Sidewinders
air-to-surface	2 x AGM-12 Bullpups
	2 x AGM-45 Shrike anti-radiation missiles
	2 x AGM-62 Walleye TV-guided glide bombs
	2 x AGM-65 Mavericks
BOMBS	6 x Rockeye-II Mark 20 cluster-bomb units (CBUs)
	6 x Rockeye Mark 7/APAM-59 CBUs
	or B43/B57/B61 nuclear bombs

GRUMMAN Ag Cat

1957

The Grumman Ag Cat biplane is a purpose-designed agricultural cropdusting (topdressing) aircraft. In the US of A, many pilots and companies were using pre-war Boeing Stearmans that had been converted for cropdusting. This was done by gutting the front cockpit and installing a hopper. The payloads were small and the aircraft were doing a job they weren't designed to do, and as a result recorded high crash rates. In an effort to rectify this, Grumman designed the Ag Cat in the mid-1950s, which turned out to be very successful. They were able to carry a 2-ton payload of fertiliser in a purpose-built hopper that sat in front of the pilot's cockpit. Some people apparently called them the 'tractor' of the aircraft world. They were powered with a 9-cylinder Pratt & Whitney R-985 Wasp Junior rotary engine that developed 450hp. To put that in perspective, the well-known Harvard aircraft is powered by a more powerful engine of the same brand and configuration, known as the Wasp, and puts out 650hp. So in reality the Ag Cat has quite a grunty motor.

Grumman had a habit of naming its models 'something' cat. The most well known being the Grumman Hellcat fighter. Apparently after much debate they named their cropduster 'Ag Cat', short for 'Agricultural Cat'. Production ran from 1955 through the 1960s.

The owners of the featured model, Peter and Marea, bought their 1965 Ag Cat four years ago. Peter was at a crossroads in his career. As a high-ranking police officer, his next step was into the upper echelons of the New Zealand Police Force, but he was not sure he wanted to take that step. While looking for a new car on Trade Me, he took a detour and had a quick look at planes for sale — not really thinking about buying anything, but, as a private pilot, he had an interest in aircraft and was just being nosy. Lo and behold, there was the Tauranga Classic Flyers' Ag Cat listed. He put it on his watch-list, and for some reason he couldn't get it out of his mind. After thinking about it for a while, he said to Marea: 'I think I've decided what I want to do.' You guessed it. He resigned from the police force, bought himself a nice franchise business to earn a living, then went and bought the Grumman Ag

Cat biplane. The hopper had been removed, and a two-seater passenger cockpit built in its place, making the plane a three-seater.

Already having a private pilot's licence, Peter started his conversion to tail-dragger aircraft on an old Piper Cub tail-dragger. (Tail-dragger refers to an aircraft having a rear tail wheel or skid, as opposed to the more modern tri-cart that features a nose wheel.) From there, he graduated to the Classic Flyers' Boeing Stearman twin open-cockpit dual-control biplane. From there, it was a hop to the single-control open-cockpit Ag Cat biplane, take a deep breath, then go fly it. All a little nerve-wracking first time up. Now with a great deal of experience flying the Ag Cat, there is nothing Peter and Marea enjoy more than donning their flying gear and taking the Ag Cat up.

I notice the plane has the name *Marea Jane* painted on the side of her, and enquire the reason. As Marea says, 'How could you not love both the man and the biplane when he names it after me?'

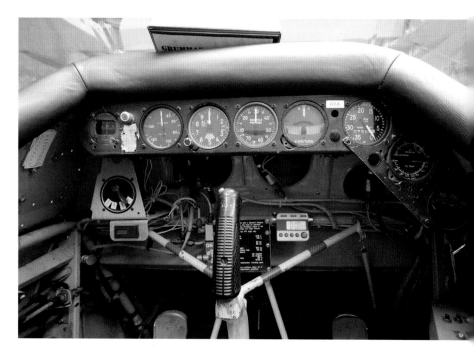

SPECIFICATIONS

CREW	1 with hopper; plus 2 passengers with hopper converted to cockpit
LENGTH	27ft 7in (8.4m)
WINGSPAN	42ft 4½in (12.92m)
HEIGHT	12ft 1in (3.68m)
WING AREA	392.7sqft (36.48sqm)
WEIGHT EMPTY	3150lb (1429kg)
WEIGHT MAX. TAKEOFF	7020lb (3184kg)
POWERPLANT	1 x Pratt & Whitney R-985 Wasp Junior radial engine, 450hp (335kW)

PERFORMANCE

MAXIMUM SPEED	147mph (237km/h)
CRUISE SPEED	125mph (200km/h)
SERVICE CEILING	13,000ft (3962m)
RATE OF CLIMB	1080ft per min (329m per min)

One of the aircraft featured here is a recent purchase by Hamilton-based Wayne Pamment. He became keen on the Nanchang while he was still a student pilot, and bought this one. He jokes: 'I had a Nanchang before I was even qualified as a pilot.' After completing his licence, he did a conversion course and got rated on the Nanchang. At the time of writing, Wayne had 20 hours' flying time in the Nanchang. So even as a newbie pilot you can get involved in the New Zealand warbird, iconic and vintage aircraft scene.

The other ones were spotted at Omaka Airfield in Blenheim. One was doing circuits and bumps. Another was refuelling, and the pilot (in his working life an international airline pilot) was most welcoming and allowed us to take cockpit and general photographs. There is no doubt that the pilots and enthusiasts involved with the different vintage aircraft clubs and warbirds scene have a great time flying these traditional aircraft.

SPECIFICATIONS

CREW	2
LENGTH	27ft 9in (8.46m)
WINGSPAN	33ft 6in (10.22m)
HEIGHT	10ft 8in (3.3m)
WEIGHT EMPTY	2414lb (1095kg)
WEIGHT LOADED	3086lb (1400kg)
POWERPLANT	1 x Zhouzhou (SMPMC) HS6A radial engine (different variants use different types), 285hp (213kW)

PERFORMANCE

MAXIMUM SPEED	185mph (300km/h)
RANGE	425 miles (700km)
SERVICE CEILING	20,500ft (6250m)

ARMAMENT

2 x 7.62mm machine guns

THE ROYAL NEW ZEALAND AIR FORCE (RNZAF)

In the dedication you would have noticed that my father and his younger brother, Bob, both served in the RNZAF during World War II. My father in Guadalcanal and New Zealand as an aircraft engineer, and Bob as a pilot in New Zealand, Canada and the United Kingdom.

As I started putting this book together, I realised that a lot of these vintage planes (or their type) actually were, at some point in time, active in our air force. I'm talking the Avro 504, the Tiger Moth, the Dominie/Rapide, the Harvards, the Kittyhawk, the DC3, the Corsair, the Oxford, the Hudson, the Avro Anson, the Catalina, the Vampire, the Venom, the Strikemaster and the Skyhawk, just for starters.

This made me stop and think about our air force, and how we tend to take it for granted. I can remember when the government of the day killed our combat wing and the Skyhawks were mothballed. The civilian joke at the time was 'Air force? What air force?!' So I decided to investigate, especially as I knew that the air force was still flying Hercules and Orion aircraft. I also knew that the first Hercules flew in 1954, and the Orion first flew in 1961. So our air force is flying vintage aircraft, right?

I gained an appointment at the airforce base at Whenuapai in West Auckland, and Marilyn and I were greeted at the gate by Squadron Leader Simon Eichelbaum. He squired us around for the day, taking us to photograph the Orion, then the Hercules. After a lovely lunch at the Officers Mess, we were able to interview Wing Commander Rob Shearer, former Commanding Officer of the Orion Squadron. That was followed by an interview with Wing Commander Andy Scott, current Commanding Officer of the Hercules Squadron. Both interviews were highly interesting and illuminating.

There is no doubt that the airframes of the Hercules and Orion are an old design, but there is also no doubt that, when they were built, both were very advanced for their day and superbly built for their individual purposes. That both models are still flying in many air forces around the world is testament to their design. The Lockheed Orion has seen 55 years of continuous use in military service around the world. The Hercules has seen 62 years in continuous military service, but even more amazing is the fact that they have been in continuous production since 1954, and are still being manufactured today. What more can you say?

Well, our three officers informed me that our Orions and our Hercules are a bit like Grandad's axe. She's the same old axe, she's only had six new axe-heads and eight new handles, but she is still Grandad's axe. So it is with the Orion and the Hercules. They have both had many extensive upgrades through their time with the RNZAF, and today the Orion is fitted out with state-of-the-art electronic surveillance equipment. The New Zealand Hercules are now the most extensively upgraded Hercules in the world, and all of the aircraft are beautifully maintained. But more of this in their individual write-ups.

I have to say that I had little idea of the aircraft, and the role that these two aircraft and their crews play in the air force. Both Marilyn and I came away from that day highly impressed with not only with the role they play, and have played, but also with the three officers we met: Wing Commander

Rob Shearer, Wing Commander Andy Scott and Squadron Leader Simon Eichelbaum. They all share a fierce pride in the RNZAF, and a fierce pride in their squadrons and their air and ground crews. That also extends to the Orion and Hercules aircraft. The missions they have accomplished left me feeling very proud of our air force and proud to call myself a New Zealander. Being a small country with a correspondingly small air force, there is no doubt that they punch well above their weight. It is something, we should all take time to think about.

LOCKHEED C-130H HERCULES

1956
(40 SQUADRON)

The origins of 40 Transport Squadron can be traced back to 1943 with the introduction of the Douglas Dakota twin-engined transports. Based at Whenuapai and flying Dakotas, Lockheed Hudsons and Lodestars, the squadron provided transport support to New Zealand and Allied personnel in the South West Pacific. The squadron was disbanded in 1947, when most of the personnel and aircraft were transferred to NAC (National Airways Corporation). It reformed in 1954 with four Handley Page Hastings CMK transports. In 1965, 40 Squadron was re-equipped with three new C-130H Hercules aircraft, with a further two in 1969. As a further part of the squadron, two B727-22QC jet transports arrived in 1981, and were replaced with two 757-200 jets in 2003.

The Hercules have been through several upgrades in their lives, with the last upgrade (one plane at a time) being the most extensive, with new wings being fitted and up-to-the-minute avionics installed. Don't expect to see analogue instruments in these old girls — they are all now digital.

The Hercules were, and still are, a perfect size for the type of work they are often engaged in. They can carry armoured vehicles, and parachute-drop them, along with heaps of supplies, paratroopers, and so on. They can also easily be converted into hospital airships. Besides being able to open their rear doors in-flight and drop large loads by parachute, they are also blessed with short landing and takeoff abilities for such a large aircraft. One of the questions I had for Wing Commander Andy Scott was what happens to the trim of the aircraft when the doors are open in-flight and when you are dropping heavy loads by parachute. The short answer to the first question is: not a lot. The doors are designed aerodynamically to open in the slipstream so as to cause minimal resistance. In fact they remain out of the airflow when open. As to the second question, it is a matter of pilot training

to hold her steady. As the heavy loads trundle to the rear of the aircraft, the nose starts to rise until she feels like she is pointing skyward, but at no time does she ever get anywhere near a stall attitude. As the loads disappear, it is just a case of levelling her out as the nose drops. These planes can carry up to 32,000lb of cargo at a time.

Our Hercules have, like the Orion, served all over the world, including Vietnam and, more latterly, Iraq, Afghanistan, East Timor, the Solomon Islands, the Balkans, Iran and Somalia, to name just a few. Wing Commander Andy Scott recalled landing on a short, dusty airstrip in Afghanistan, dropping off supplies at the frontline, taking off again, then two weeks later he was flying the same aircraft over Antarctica. So they certainly get around. In fact, besides being the most updated Hercules in the world, our aircraft also have some of the highest recorded airframe hours in the Western world.

The crew of a Hercules consists of two pilots, two loadmasters and either one or two flight engineers. The number of flight engineers depends on where the mission is, and how long it goes for. Wing Commander Andy Scott reminded me that, although the Hercules has been upgraded, she is still using 1960s-designed engines. He can remember having to shut down an engine in an out-of-the-way place due to a bleed air leak. He put her down on a short-range strip, and the flight engineers climbed out to have a look.

They discovered that a particular seal had failed. One of the engineers said, 'Hang on a minute, boss, I think I've got one of those in my bag of tricks.' An hour later, they were flying on all four engines. As Andy says, they are a great aircraft for what we use them for, and where else in the world, in any air force, would you find crew like that? It's the old Kiwi can-do attitude coming to the rescue. (You've just got to love these guys, don't you?)

We were treated to a great display of the Hercules' abilities at the recent Warbirds Over Wanaka airshow. It was pretty impressive.

The 'Hercs' are scheduled for replacement around 2020–2023, and a number of aircraft are in the melting pot for selection. But do you know what? If we really want an aircraft that can do everything a Hercules can do, then it would be hard to go past replacing a Hercules with another Hercules ...

SPECIFICATIONS

CREW	6
LENGTH	97ft 9in (29.8m)
WINGSPAN	132ft 7in (40.5m)
HEIGHT	38ft 3in (11.7m)
WEIGHT EMPTY	77,000lb (34,927kg)
WEIGHT LOADED	155,000lb (70,307kg)
CARGO CAPACITY	92 ground troops *or* 64 paratroopers and equipment *or* 70 stretchers *or* 6 cargo pallets
POWERPLANT	4 x Allison T56-A-15 engines, 4910hp (366kW)

PERFORMANCE

MAXIMUM SPEED	373mph (600km/h)
CRUISE SPEED	344mph (555km/h)
RANGE	4623 miles (7440km) empty; 2548 miles (4100km) with 28,000lb (12,700kg) payload
SERVICE CEILING	42,000ft (12,802m)
RATE OF CLIMB	1830ft per min (9.3m per sec)

LOCKHEED P-3K2 ORION

1962
(5 SQUADRON)

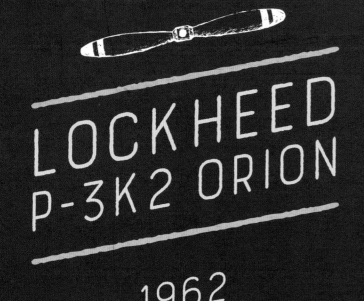

The Royal New Zealand Air Force (RNZAF) operates six P-3K2 Orion aircraft to meet New Zealand's airborne surveillance requirements. 5 Squadron was formed in 1941. Based in Fiji with first Vincents, then four elderly Short Singapore flying boats, the squadron provided long-range maritime patrols for the region. Briefly disbanded in 1942, it was reformed in 1944 with Catalina flying boats. The field of operations was from Espiritu Santo to the Admiralty Islands. Following World War II, the squadron relocated to Lauthala Bay (Fiji). In 1953, the Catalinas were retired, and Short Sunderland flying boats took over. In 1966, five new Orion P-3B aircraft were purchased by the RNZAF. Over time, several further modernisation enhancements of all avionics and electronic surveillance equipment has since taken place, and our Orions are now running up-to-the-minute equipment in these departments. A sixth Orion was purchased from the Royal Australian Air Force in 1985. In the mid-1980s, they were upgraded to P-3K from P-3B, and since then have been upgraded to P-3K2 specs.

The Orions are used for maritime surveillance, maritime reconnaissance, exclusive economic zone patrols, anti-submarine warfare, anti-surface unit warfare, and search and rescue. These aircraft are quite amazing. They have a top speed of 466mph (750km/h), and can cruise comfortably at 391mph (630km/h). They can extend their airborne time quite considerably by cruising at a very respectable speed on three engines with the fourth shut down. If on anti-submarine patrol, they are further able to extend flying time by cutting back to two engines, so that they can 'loiter' in the designated patrol destination area for a few hours, cruising at just 160 knots. With search and rescue, their systems are so good that if a Pacific Islands fishing boat has no signalling device but does

have a motor, albeit broken down, the Orion can still often pick them up by getting an 'echo' off the steel in the motor. All of our Orions are able to be fully armed, so are in fact a war plane as opposed to just being a reconnaissance aircraft.

RNZAF Orions have served all around the world, including flying 142 anti-terrorist missions in the Gulf of Oman and the Arabian Sea in 2003 and 2004 as part of an international coalition of countries. They have also flown to Antarctica.

The crew on an Orion consists of the pilot, co-pilot, two flight engineers, two navigators (including a tactical air co-ordinator), an air electronics officer, four electronics operators and an ordinance crewmember. (The Orions can carry up to 21 personnel.) Each member has specific functions to perform, with the tactical air co-ordinator liaising between pilots, navigation and electronic surveillance on each mission.

Our Orions are actually kept pretty busy, with the one we were going to photograph deployed on a mission the same day (before we could photograph her). The second one we photographed as she left on another urgent deployment.

The Orions are lovely to fly, very manoeuvrable and surprisingly fast, according to former Commanding Officer, Wing Commander Rob Shearer.

SPECIFICATIONS

CREW	12
LENGTH	36m (117ft)
WINGSPAN	30.4m (99ft)
HEIGHT	38ft 8in (11.8m)
WEIGHT EMPTY	30,450kg (67,000lb)
WEIGHT LOADED	54,950kg (127,500lb)
POWERPLANT	4 x Allison T56-A 14 engines, 4600hp (3430kW)

PERFORMANCE

MAXIMUM SPEED	466mph (750km/h)
CRUISE SPEED	391mph (630km/h)
FERRY RANGE	4412 miles approx (7100km)
TYPICAL PERFORMANCE	Radius of action of 1850km (1150 miles) with 4 hr on station; endurance 15 hr with 2 engines shut down
SERVICE CEILING	28,300ft (8625m)
RATE OF CLIMB	3140ft per min (16m per sec)

ARMAMENT

Classified

BAC 167 STRIKEMASTER

1967

I first saw a brace of Strikemasters flying at Ardmore. I had not really noticed these aircraft prior to this point, although they had flown in the Royal New Zealand Air Force (RNZAF) for a number of years. The British-built Strikemaster was essentially a jet Provost T Mk 5 which was modified with an uprated engine, wing hardpoints, strengthened airframe, new navigational equipment and communications, shortened landing gear and a revised fuel system. They were also fitted with uprated ejection seats. Marketed as a light attack insurgency aircraft, most were in fact sold to air forces around the world as a trainer aircraft. They first flew in 1967. The RNZAF acquired 16 Strikemasters in 1972. In 1981, the RNZAF reduced their use, after discovering cracking in the main wing structures. Considering the expense of re-winging them, the air force retired them in 1994, replacing them with the Aermacchi MB339-CB trainers.

While none now fly with air forces, the Strikemasters (affectionately known as 'Blunty' in New Zealand) have found a new lease of life with Warbird fraternities around the world. Of the 146 built, 15-plus are still flying.

In New Zealand, both restored Strikemasters are owned by businessman Brett Nicolls. Brett was brought up in the jet age, and it is these aircraft that fire his enthusiasm, rather than the older propeller-driven aircraft. Brett has gained his commercial licence and is racking up hours on the Strikemasters. He has two pilots who fly these machines for show displays, and he has also set up a company in Auckland where you can go for jet fighter rides. Both jets are ex-RNZAF Strikemasters that were sold to Australia. Brett bought them back again; one in 2010, the other in 2014. They are still wearing their original style of paint and numbers of the RNZAF, and still look really good.

It is just awesome to see these little beauties flying, and to hear the noise of their beautiful jet engine on song.

For the younger generation, the jets are certainly a more relevant warbird to which they can relate, but they can still stir the blood of my generation as well. I have been fortunate to see these two aircraft flying in display a number of times, including in tight formation with two Vampire jets.

SPECIFICATIONS

CREW	2 (pilot, co-pilot)
LENGTH	33ft 8.5in (10.27m)
WINGSPAN	36ft 10in (11.23m)
HEIGHT	10ft 11.5in (3.34m)
WEIGHT EMPTY	6195lb (2810kg)
WEIGHT LOADED	9303lb (4219kg)
POWERPLANT	1 x Rolls Royce Viper Mk. 535 turbojet engine, 3140lbf (15kN)

PERFORMANCE

MAXIMUM SPEED	481mph (834km/h)
STALL SPEED	95mph (158km/h) flaps down
RANGE	1382 miles (2224km)
SERVICE CEILING	40,000ft (12,200m)
RATE OF CLIMB	5250ft per min (26.7m per sec)

ARMAMENT

GUNS	2 x 7.62mm Nato machine guns
BOMBS	4 (2 per wing) capacity of 3000lb (1364kg) bombs, machine gun pods, air-to-ground rocket pods, fuel drop tanks

YAKOVLEV
YAK-52

1976

canopy reminds one of the Harvard and Chipmunk set-up. Her instrument panel and seats are like those of earlier aircraft, and she is powered by a 9-cylinder radial engine. She just has the look of a World War II fighter. The long undercart is designed for the long-grassed rough airstrips that are found in Russia and surrounding countries. This helps absorb the bumps and keeps the propeller above the grass.

Since the fall of the Soviet Union in the early 1990s, Yaks have been finding their way to the West. Of the approximately 1800 built so far, many of them are now in the United States, the United Kingdom, New Zealand, Australia and other Western countries.

They are a good, robust, fun aircraft to own and fly, they have the look of an old warbird, and they are generally well priced in comparison to other warbird stock.

They are fantastic to watch in full flight, especially with a group of them. We watched them take off in formation, two to three wide, then fly across the airfield in a formation of nine. As if this wasn't enough, we then watched them complete a full aerobatic loop in a tight formation of nine aircraft. A new world record, I believe. They then split into two groups, performing synchronised aerobatics. Great fun to watch!

Given our journey with the Yak-52s, it would have been a crime not to include them in this book. They are now an iconic aircraft in New Zealand and totally accepted in the warbird scene.

SPECIFICATIONS

CREW	2
LENGTH	25ft 5in (7.745m)
WINGSPAN	30ft 6in (9.30m)
HEIGHT	8ft 10in (2.70m)
WEIGHT EMPTY	2238lb (1015kg)
WEIGHT LOADED	2877lb (1305kg)
POWERPLANT	1 x Vedeneyev M-14P 9-cylinder radial engine, 360hp (268kW)

PERFORMANCE

MAXIMUM SPEED	177mph (285km/h)
CRUISE SPEED	118mph (190km/h)
STALL SPEED	54mph (87km/h)
RANGE	341 miles (550km)
SERVICE CEILING	13,125ft (4000m)
RATE OF CLIMB	1378ft per min (7.0m per sec)

NEW ZEALAND AVIATION MUSEUMS

Some aircraft that are housed at particular museums are flown regularly. Others are held in posterity for future generations to enjoy and wonder over. These latter aircraft are static in display. There are always two schools of thought on static and flying aircraft. The statics are safe forever, but we can only stand and look and admire and wonder at them. The airworthy craft give our generation a view of these iconic aircraft in flight, which is absolutely fantastic, but they fly always with the risk of something going wrong, always giving rise to a further risk of a crash or fire, either of which could totally destroy the aircraft. I have to admit I absolutely love the thrill of seeing these old aircraft in the air, but also deeply appreciate the static aircraft, and the reason they are on static display.

I have visited all of the museums listed here, and there is no doubt in my mind that our aviation museums and the aircraft they display represent New Zealand aviation and vintage military aviation exceptionally well, and each and every one is well worth visiting.

AUCKLAND WAR
MEMORIAL
INSTITUTE AND
MUSEUM

The Auckland War Memorial Institute and Museum is what I term a general museum. It has a large range of artefacts and New Zealand history in its environs. In terms of aviation, it has a small area dedicated to the air force, and two aircraft in particular. It has one of the last Spitfires ever built, and also the very rare Japanese Mitsubishi Zero featured earlier in this book. The Mitsubishi Zero story is great (see page 186). The Spitfire was gifted by a grateful Great Britain to the Auckland War Memorial Institute and Museum in 1956. The aircraft delivery was arranged by New Zealander Sir Keith Park, who was the Air Force Commander at the time of the Battle of Britain. The Spitfire was built in 1945, but never saw combat. It was commissioned in 1951, and flew just 638 flying hours before being gifted to New Zealand. It is a MK XVI model and is powered by a Packard Merlin 266 engine, as opposed to the more common Rolls Royce Merlin engine. The displays of the two fighters are great, and it is well worth taking the time to view these two historic aircraft.

MUSEUM OF TRANSPORT AND TECHNOLOGY (MOTAT), AUCKLAND

At Western Springs, near central Auckland, is the Museum of Transport and Technology, commonly known as 'MOTAT'. This museum covers, through the ages, the transport and technical developments of products and early houses used in New Zealand and by New Zealanders. Around the corner from the museum, just past the Auckland Zoo, is the aviation part of the museum. It is fronted by a massive hangar that houses some incredible aircraft, including the Solent flying boat (see page 226) and the featured Lancaster, and one of the Hudson bombers (see pages 206 and 174, respectively). Along with these are some great civil and topdressing vintage aircraft, as well as some vintage warbirds.

Many more planes are under restoration, and on Wednesday mornings the museum opens up the back hangars to volunteers, who come in and work on the restorations. MOTAT has developed relationships with aviation groups, like Friends of the Solent and the Bomber Command Association, and both supply members to talk to visitors and carry out restoration work.

Again, like the other aviation museums, MOTAT is well worth the visit. Some of the aircraft are incredibly rare, with the Solent being the only Mk IV model left in the world!

**VISITOR CENTRE
NEW ZEALAND
WARBIRDS ASSOCIATION,
ARDMORE, AUCKLAND**

The New Zealand Warbirds Association is the national umbrella body responsible for the safe management of the operating environment for ex-military and vintage aircraft in New Zealand. Their membership consists of aircraft owners, commercial pilots, ex-service personnel and aviation enthusiasts. Many of the aircraft that come under their auspices are owned by syndicates, so as to share the costs of maintaining and flying these beautiful aircraft. The planes are domiciled across New Zealand, but many of them are located at Ardmore Aerodrome in south Auckland. At Ardmore, one can find the headquarters of the New Zealand Warbirds Association, along with their museum.

The museum has an extensive aeronautical library and a stunning photographic display and written history of some of the planes and their war history. The main hangar has a few static displays, but mostly a revolving display of members' vintage war planes. Around the aerodrome are many hangars holding other warbirds, along with businesses that specialise in restorations and giving warbird rides. The aircraft range from Tiger Moth biplanes that the air force used for pilot training in World War II, through to fighter planes used in the same war, and on to jet fighters and trainers used by the air force in later years. Weekends often see these planes in the air. They also have mini airshows at different times, and these feature some spectacular flying.

The day we were there, we saw jet fighters along with the iconic Harvard and Mustang fighter planes from World War II. Also present were a couple of less-known, but very interesting aircraft, one used for clandestine flights into France, landing supplies and spies onto short landing strips.

The museum is well worth being on your itinerary, if you are interested in these old aircraft.

CLASSIC FLYERS, MOUNT MAUNGANUI

Housed at the Tauranga Airport at Mount Maunganui, the Classic Flyers museum is run by a charitable trust, with much of the income derived from donations and fundraising. Much of the restoration work on aircraft that are acquired or donated to the trust is carried out by volunteers, with many of the personnel who show people around the museum also being enthusiastic volunteers. The museum is fronted by a very vintage-aircraft-orientated café, with the entrance to the museum being through the café to a memorabilia museum shop. This shop is very interesting and leads to the main display hangar. Upstairs are conference rooms that businesses can hire.

The museum was started by a group of local vintage aviators who approached the local council about using an abandoned World War II hangar on the airfield. As maintenance of the hangar was costing the council money, they were quite keen on the idea. However, when a survey of the hangar was carried out, it was found to be in a very sad state, and was condemned and pulled down. Nonetheless, the council came back to the airmen and said that they could see potential in the museum, and that it would be a good tourist attraction. A feasibility study was subsequently carried out, a site was chosen at the gateway to the airport, and things proceeded. Andrew Gormlie, now a major shareholder in the trust, is the current CEO and the driving force behind the museum. It has to be run on a profitable basis to pay its overheads, and to create money to continue to grow its exhibits and maintain its airworthy craft. It has always been policy to have airworthy craft and to give, where and when possible, live vintage airshows. It is all about giving the visitor a memory they won't forget.

The displays featured here are both static aircraft and airworthy aircraft, and range from military to civilian, and from biplanes through to World War II aircraft to jet fighters. There are historic photographs, and aero engines are also on display. A second and third hangar, one of which houses a Grumman Avenger under restoration, completes the museum, along with outside exhibits. This is a museum well worth visiting, and, along with some of the museums mentioned so far, has flying examples and a band of enthusiastic pilots who fly the aircraft when they can. Every now and again the museum runs mini airshows, which are absolutely fantastic and are a really great way to spend a day. If you happen to pass through Tauranga, make sure you take the time to visit. You will not be disappointed.

AVIATION HERITAGE TRUST, MASTERTON

If you are a keen aviation enthusiast, or even have a general interest in aircraft, then a trip to the Aviation Heritage Trust's collection housed in a museum hangar at Hood Aerodrome in Masterton is really worthwhile. Even if your interest in aircraft is low, I am sure you would still enjoy this museum. Along with some very old motorcycles, a World War I double-decker troop-carrier bus, the original Chitty Chitty Bang Bang car, plus a World War II Corsair and a World War II Kittyhawk fighter plane, resides a most incredible collection of World War I aircraft. In fact, it is believed to be one of the largest collections of World War I aircraft in the world. If you have read this book, then many of the featured planes you have read about in previous pages are housed in this living museum. There are also many aircraft that have not been featured in this book. Some are static displays, but many are airworthy and are often flown.

Visiting this museum allows you to get up close and personal with these unique aircraft. Many are old planes that have been meticulously restored, while others are reproduction builds that are so authentic and exact to the original specifications that it would be impossible to tell the difference between an original and a replica or reproduction model. Some aircraft are replicas that have been imported. Most of these planes have been built and restored by The Vintage Aviator Ltd, and all of the examples are maintained for the museum by The Vintage Aviator Ltd. The museum is open on weekends. If you are passing through Masterton, make sure you take the time to take a guided tour around these unique aircraft of yesteryear.

OMAKA
AVIATION HERITAGE
CENTRE, BLENHEIM

Whether you are into aircraft or not, this museum is a must for your bucket-list. It is simply superb. Not only does it house both static and some airworthy vintage and reproduction World War I aircraft and a huge amount of memorabilia, but it captures beautifully the essence of what it must have been like to live through that terrible war. The Omaka Aviation Heritage Centre is run by the New Zealand Aviation Centre Trust, and was born through a love of vintage aviation by a small group of people in the Blenheim area. Sir Peter Jackson, a keen collector of World War I aircraft and memorabilia, offered his collection to the trust, and along the way brought the displays to life with incredible sets created by the internationally famous Weta Workshop and Wingnut Films. The Vintage Aviator Ltd was responsible for creating some of the reproduction aircraft, with the majority of other aircraft sourced from around the world.

The exhibits have been put together by creating life-like scenes around the aircraft, to transport you back to World War I. There are creative scenes based on real-life events, there are aircraft-manufacturing scenes, and the range of World War I aircraft is fantastic.

This museum is an absolute credit to the members of the trust and to all those involved in its creation and the ongoing running of the museum. The exhibition is appropriately called Knights of the Sky. It is a jewel in Blenheim's crown, and is a must-see for New Zealanders and overseas tourists alike.

As we have been putting this book together, the good folk at Omaka Heritage have been busy putting together a stunning new display of World War II aircraft. This new exhibition, called Dangerous Skies, tells the aviation story of World War II, and opens in 2016. Like the Knights of the Skies exhibition, Dangerous Skies transports you to different parts of the world during World War II, especially picking up countries where New Zealand airmen were involved with the fighting. Not to be missed!

AIR FORCE MUSEUM OF NEW ZEALAND, WIGRAM

This is a beautifully presented museum, both inside and out. Set in the remains of the historic airforce base, it boasts a beautiful main display area, with a display workshop area out to the rear. They have an amazing range of aircraft on static display, from the early days of the air force right through to the fighter jets of later years. The newly restored Oxford advanced trainer bomber of World War II is, to my way of thinking, one of the jewels in their crown. It has been beautifully restored back to its original configuration, and is just stunning. The Royal Air Force DC3 that was converted for Queen Elizabeth II's visit to New Zealand in 1953 is absolutely beautiful inside, and in 1953 would have been the height of luxury — indeed, 'fit for a queen'.

Besides the fantastic array of aircraft, they also have lots of memorabilia and many stories of different Kiwi airforce personnel who distinguished themselves through the ages. The stories make for great reading, and again reinforce the Kiwi can-do attitude, and the courage and fortitude of these particular men and women.

This museum is an essential on your aviation visiting list. The staff are fantastic and very knowledgeable. They are also immensely proud of their display, and it shows, which is great for the visitor.

ASHBURTON AVIATION MUSEUM

This museum is an eye-opener. Set in a couple of hangars at Ashburton Airport, at first glance it looks nothing in particular, with just a small sign above the door. It is staffed by volunteers and is very laid-back. However, what is inside will knock your socks off. Besides the unusual Air Truck topdresser, there are quite a number of vintage civil aircraft. They also have a great selection of early jet fighters, including not only a couple of Vampires but also its predecessor, a Gloster Meteor — the very first jet fighter of the Allies, a model that actually saw service at the end of World War II. I never for a minute expected to see a Gloster Meteor in New Zealand, let alone in Ashburton! That plane alone makes this museum worth a visit. It really is another must-see museum.

WARBIRDS
AND WHEELS
MUSEUM, WANAKA

Fronted by a really nice vintage-styled café, this museum features both vintage aeroplanes and cars and motorcycles. If you are like me, you will really enjoy both facets of this museum. The selection of aircraft is very interesting, and dates from World War I aircraft through to jet fighters. A selection of motorcycles (many of them from my teenage years) will take the eye, and some of the cars are absolute standouts. They have a great selection of American Packards from the 1920s and 1930s (very rare, very expensive and very Art Deco), along with Cadillacs and Fords. If your interests run to old aircraft, old cars and old motorcycles, the whole museum will certainly have you drooling. What more can you ask of a museum? With this one, you kind of want to pack it up and take it home with you. No doubt you will gather from the aforementioned script that this museum is unmissable.

CROYDON
AVIATION HERITAGE
CENTRE, MANDEVILLE

Based in the South Island at the old Mandeville Airfield, a few kilometres north of Gore, is the beautifully presented Croydon Aviation Heritage Centre. Most of the exhibits are airworthy, with some that can also be chartered for a flight. At the time I visited, they had many aircraft from the 1930s, some of which have been individually featured in this book.

There was the De Havilland Rapide, also known as the Dominie (one of only four in the world still flying). Behind it is another Rapide under restoration. Four Tiger Moths, a Fox Moth, a very rare De Havilland Dragonfly and an old Auster were also in residence. Other planes were dotted around, including an Aermacchi jet fighter trainer.

This is a great museum, and I was so glad I had taken the time to check it out. Like the others, it is well worth a visit. I keep being blown away by the aircraft we have here in New Zealand, and Mandeville is no exception.

NEW ZEALAND AIRSHOWS

In New Zealand, we have three airshows of note. Two are international shows. Warbirds Over Wanaka spans the Easter holiday period, and is run every second year. The other international show is the Classic Fighters Omaka Airshow, which is also run over the Easter break, but on an alternate year from Warbirds Over Wanaka. Both offer a fantastic spectacle for audiences, and are very much a 'show' in terms of their presentation. They are designed to entertain. The third show, Wings Over Wairarapa, is a more recent show, and is generally run in February on the same year as the Classic Fighters Omaka Airshow. Wings Over Wairarapa is growing every year. All three airshows are well and truly worth attending. They really show off New Zealand vintage and iconic aviation to both New Zealanders and international visitors alike, and their increasing popularity cannot be denied.

WINGS OVER WAIRARAPA

Wings Over Wairarapa celebrates its tenth biennial airshow in February 2017, the first time the show will be held outside the traditional Wellington Anniversary weekend. With crowds of nearly 25,000 at the previous two shows, the Wings team is looking forward to attracting another large crowd to the Wairarapa. 'It's a long way from the 9000 people who showed up at the first event in 1999,' says Tom Williams, airshow director, original organiser, and chair of the New Zealand Sport and Vintage Aviation Society (SVAS). 'Wings Over Wairarapa began with an suggestion from a friend of mine,' continues Tom. 'I was sitting on a plane with Tim Wallis [founder of Warbirds Over Wanaka] on the way to Korea, and Tim said: Tom, "You should run an airshow." And so we did.'

The 'we' is the team from SVAS, many of whom are still heavily involved in the show today. 'The vision was to get a few dollars so we could preserve our vintage aviation and fly some of our old aeroplanes, but it's grown exponentially,' Tom says.

In 2005, SVAS realised that the air show could reach another level, but to do this they needed professional event management support and advice, and so Liz Pollock, an experienced event manager, joined the team. Liz grew the event with each subsequent airshow, so that the range of display aircraft, entertainment and food, visitor parking and traffic management all improved year on year. Her final show, before she stood down, was perhaps her finest and proudest achievement during her time with Wings Over Wairarapa. As for the crowd, it was the most successful and most memorable, both for aviation buffs and the general public alike. It was of course Wings 2013, which featured the Mosquito.

'The Mosquito was one of the fastest operational aircraft in World War II, and the only one to be constructed almost entirely of wood. Its significance to World War II history is not to be underestimated. The legendary Mosquito has a fond place in the hearts of Australian and New Zealand airmen, with about 250 aircraft being built in Australia during the war,' says Tom, who was instrumental in securing the Mosquito after first meeting its owner, Mr Jerry Yagen, in 2008 at the Warbirds Over Wanaka airshow.

The Mosquito, nicknamed the 'Wooden Wonder', first flew in November 1941, and became operational in 1942. They were faster than the Spitfire with a top speed of 366mph, powered by twin Merlin engines, meaning bombing missions were dramatically shortened, lessening the risk to pilots. Their versatility meant they were also used in other roles, including daytime tactical bombing, high-altitude night-bombing and photo reconnaissance. Produced in huge factories, around 6000 Mosquitos rolled off the British production line; others were built in Canada and Australia. Around 80 ended up in New Zealand and were used by the Royal New Zealand Air Force (RNZAF).

It really was a once-in-a-lifetime opportunity to see this unique aircraft fly and line up alongside 12 other de Havilland aircraft, which ranged from an early World War I biplane, the DH.5, to the DH Vampire jet. The organisers still get comments and questions about whether there will be another.

Wings is held at the Hood Aerodrome, a fantastic asset for Masterton at the south end of town. The aerodrome began when the Wairarapa and Ruahine Aero Club received a donation of land for a Masterton airfield on South Road near the Waingawa River. Working-bees were organised to clear the stony land, and on 14 March 1931 the first official North Island Air Pageant was held at the new airfield, with 33 aircraft attending. During the air pageant, Masterton's airfield was officially named 'Hood Aerodrome' after Captain George Hood, a Masterton-born aviation pioneer who had died trying to fly the first Tasman Sea crossing, along with Lieutenant John Robert Moncrieff, in January 1928.

The Hood Aerodrome website tells us that 1940 saw the RNZAF occupy Hood Aerodrome, with more land bought by the government to increase the airfield's size, and three runways being constructed. By April 1942, 14 Squadron had re-formed at the aerodrome, using American-built Harvard

trainers and P-40 Kittyhawk fighters. Later, in 1943, 14 Squadron left to fight the Japanese in the South Pacific. With the cessation of war in 1945, aircraft returned to Hood and the aero club began flying again, using Tiger Moths, Proctors and Auster aircraft.

Fast-forward to the present day, and the planning is well underway for Wings Over Wairarapa 2017. General manager Jenny Gasson talks about extending the success of the drone programme which was implemented in 2015. Working closely with Callaghan Innovation and the Royal Aeronautical Society, they have also hosted a very successful conference and trade event which saw over 10,000 people attend in two days. Governance and management of the event was taken over by the Wings Over Wairarapa Community Trust Board after the 2011 event, although SVAS remains heavily involved.

Wings Over Wairarapa is known for being a family-friendly air event with lots of activities for both aviation buffs and people who are just looking for a great day out. It is a big day on the Wairarapa region's calendar, drawing people from overseas and out of town.

Based on material supplied by Jenny Gasson, Warbirds Over Wairarapa general manager.

CLASSIC
FIGHTERS OMAKA
AIRSHOW

The biennial Classic Fighters Airshow held at the historic Omaka Airfield in Marlborough takes place on the 'odd' Easters every second year, alternating with the Warbirds Over Wanaka event.

The Omaka events began as simple fly-ins for owners and enthusiasts, as early as 1995, when an event for classic machines took place in March. Two years later, it was decided to scale the event up to welcome the New Zealand Warbirds Association to Omaka as a joint Easter fly-in weekend. This followed again in 1999, and grew a little more, attracting as it did a lot of interest from the public. At this point the local vintage aviation community decided, with the blessing of the Omaka Airfield owners, the Marlborough Aero Club, to host a full-blown airshow.

The move from casual fly-in to public airshow did not happen without a lot of thought and not a small amount of foreboding. As organiser Graham Orphan told the group at the time: 'We have now just replaced an aviation event with an entertainment event.' From well before the first show, the team wanted to avoid creating something that would mirror events that had been held before. They wanted to show people things that were unexpected, things they wouldn't have seen before.

The Classic Fighters Airshow had to be different. Because there was no large resident collection of exotic aircraft, they needed to be more creative if they were to deliver a quality show. This problem was addressed in three ways. Firstly, the show would bring in a couple of aeroplanes from overseas. One of these was a CAC Boomerang loaned for the occasion by Lynette Zuccoli of Toowoomba, Queensland; another was a replica Bristol fighter made available by owner/builder Ed Storo of Memphis, Tennessee. The second solution involved presenting different groups of aeroplanes together. The Bristol fighter was put together with two Omaka-resident World War I machines: a Fokker Triplane built by Stuart Tantrum, and a Sopwith Camel recently imported by Sir Peter Jackson and also prepared for flight in New Zealand by Stuart. Coupled with these three flyable World War I aircraft were a static replica Fokker D.VIII, a couple of World War I tanks, and a two-storey French château, all of these props produced locally by the airshow team. There was even a German observation balloon flying above the château. It was New Zealand's first World War I battle tableau, and the crowd just loved it. This set the scene for future Classic Fighters events, in which the acting out of stories of World War I battles in the air and on the ground have always played an import role.

The third way to make the event unique was to theme each show, so that each airshow had a distinct theme. Many of these have been geographically or campaign-influenced — North Africa, Italy, France — providing wonderful opportunities for the highly creative props teams to really go crazy. They have built the Arc de Triomphe, pyramids, a full-size Stuka dive-bomber, a wonderful replica of the Eiffel Tower that was over 20 metres tall and required engineering sign-off and a light on the top (by the Civil Aviation Authority). The Italian theme was especially challenging with no Italian aeroplanes to access. The team built a replica of the monastery at Monte Cassino up on a hillside overlooking the airfield. This edifice was 60 metres long, 30 metres wide and 20 metres tall — before it was attacked by fighter bombers and began to collapse. While still in Italy, visitors also got to watch a gondola race across Venice's grassy canals (the very convincing gondolas were built around farm quad-bikes). And then there was the unusual Bristol freighter cargo: in this case, the Omaka Bristol, the only operational example in the world, taxied to

a halt, opened its large mouth, and regurgitated over a dozen Vespa motor-scooters.

Some of the more challenging prop builds have included the full-scale V-2 rocket with its Meillerwagen trailer, which allowed the missile to be hoisted into launch position (20 metres tall), ignite its rocket motors, and then begin lifting off, climbing only a couple of metres before the strafing Spitfires and Kittyhawks hit their target and the huge weapon toppled, exploding on its way to the ground, and again as it crashed to the grass. More recently, several V-1 rockets were also produced, complete with launch ramp. Each was strafed and exploded, except for one which succeeded in actually launching into the sky and flying several times down the crowd line to an astonished audience — a world airshow first, and one to be regularly repeated at every Classic Fighters show!

Of course the stars of the show are the aircraft themselves, and the Classic Fighters team likes to always provide some new, unseen aircraft and a large number of show planes. For example, the 2015 event featured around 100 exotic aircraft, and the final warbird fly-by parade showcased a carpet of 30 fighters, Harvards, Yaks and Nanchangs casting their shadows over the field, followed by the Omaka-based Avro Anson Mk 1, the only one of its type flying in the world, which deployed a sea of red poppies in an emotional finale to the show.

The airshow team remains an enthusiastic, professional, fun-loving group, who volunteer their time. Their penchant for the unexpected has led to the hashtag #OnlyatOmaka becoming the unwritten slogan for the show.

Among the highlights of the show over the years have been some significant aircraft debuts, quite apart from those already listed at the first show way back in 2001. Perhaps the most significant of these was the Focke-Wulf Fw 190A8 of the Omaka-based Chariots of Fire Fighter Collection. There had never been an Fw 190 display at an event south of the Equator, and at the time of writing, this remains the case. The Fw 190 made a brief debut at the 2011 airshow, participated fully in the 2013 show, and performed again at the 2015 event, where it unfortunately suffered some damage in a landing mishap. It is set to return in 2017. Another first in 2015 was the sight of no fewer than three Spitfires in the air at once, again a sight not seen anywhere

else in the Southern Hemisphere since the war years. The star of that group was the just-completed Spitfire Mk XIVe, also a resident of Omaka. A number of the significant World War I aircraft debuts at Omaka have been courtesy of The Vintage Aviator Ltd (TVAL), whose craftsman have built a reputation for recreating entire aircraft, including engines, wheels, instruments, etc, to the highest standard. Also thanks to the TVAL team, and something really surprising for most, has been the mass formation of Fokker Triplanes, the 2015 show revealing the amazing 'Fokker Flight' of nine World War I Fokker aeroplanes, comprising eight Dr.1 Triplanes and a solitary D.VII. Going back even earlier, the 'Pioneer Race' was launched in 2015, bringing together three 1910-era aeroplanes with cars and penny-farthing bicycles of the same period to present a 'Magnificent Men'-style tableau, which the crowd just loved. Once again, the surprise of seeing something unexpected hit the target as it does every time!

Based on material supplied by Graham Orphan, Airshow Chairman.

WARBIRDS OVER WANAKA

Warbirds Over Wanaka International Airshow has an enviable reputation as one of the world's premier warbirds airshows, and is held in one of the most stunning settings in the world. The biennial airshow was the brainchild of New Zealand business and aviation pioneer Sir Tim Wallis. By the late 1980s Tim had already amassed a world-class collection of warbird aircraft, and the airshow came out of his desire to share them with other aircraft enthusiasts.

The first airshow, in 1988, was called Warbirds On Parade, and attracted 14,000 to the small Wanaka airfield in Central Otago. From the first airshow's single day, the event has grown to four days — practice day on the Friday, full airshow on the Saturday and Sunday, and a Rides Day on the Monday. The airshow now attracts a crowd of around 50,000 people every second Easter. While the majority of those attending are from New Zealand, each airshow also attracts several thousand international visitors, particularly from Australia. Warbirds Over Wanaka is definitely a 'bucket-list' event for many vintage aircraft enthusiasts.

In the early days, the airshow was run under the auspices of the Alpine Deer Company, owned and operated by Tim, but in 2006 ownership of the event passed to the Warbirds Over Wanaka Community Trust. The Trust's vision is to 'aspire to be the best Warbirds airshow in the world' while its mission is 'to educate through the celebration of aviation past and present'.

Over the years some of the world's most remarkable warbirds aircraft and pilots have graced the skies of Wanaka. The very early days of aviation have been marked with aircraft such as the Bleriot XI and the incredible Vintage Aviator collection of beautiful World War I aircraft. World War II aircraft form the core of Warbirds Over Wanaka displays, and over the years all manner of aircraft have displayed, including the Spitfire, the Hurricane, the Corsair, the Sea Fury, the P-40 Kittyhawk (with guns firing), the P-51 Mustang, the Grumman Avenger, the Catalina, the Avro Anson, the Me-109bf, the Buchon Me-109, the Yak-3 and a gaggle of Polikarpovs, just to mention a few.

Then there are all manner of other aerial displays, from jets to helicopters and gliders to skydiving. To top it all off, Warbirds Over Wanaka is the only civilian airshow in New Zealand which attracts a significant military component. The Royal New Zealand Air Force has been a stalwart of the airshow for many years, showing off the full range of New Zealand military aircraft over that time. In 2016, a record four air forces displayed: the Royal New Zealand Air Force, the Royal Australian Air Force, the United States Air Force, and the French Air Force. Over the years, highlights of visiting military aircraft have included the Royal Australian Air Force's F1-11 and Hornets, and the US Air Force's C-17 Globemaster.

Warbirds Over Wanaka is about more than just the aircraft. The extensive ground displays mean that it is very hard to take everything in in one day. More than 100 local re-enactors also set up camp at the airfield, and stage realistic mock battles. The pyrotechnics and props team is always coming up with new and innovative ways to light up the skies and keep the crowd guessing. Add in a big range of trade displays, vehicle displays, and great local food and beverages, and you have the recipe for one of the best weekends possible, held against one of the most beautiful backdrops in the world.

Based on material supplied by Ed Taylor, airshow general manager.

MERCURY BAY AREA SCHOOL — TOMORROW'S AVIATION ENTHUSIASTS

This story is one that almost defies belief. Jim, a retired aircraft engineer and pilot, moved to the small seaside resort of Whitianga, on the Coromandel Peninsula's east coast in New Zealand, and naturally joined the local aero club. However, the club was concerned that all of its members were getting older and that it needed to attract younger people into the club. Jim suggested that maybe they could approach the school and see whether they could attract some of the senior students. The idea grew into: 'Why not suggest they build a kitset plane and be given the opportunity to learn to fly?' Jim approached the principal, John Wright, who enthusiastically got behind the idea. The upshot was that Jim organised a Van's RV-12 kitset, found a place to build the plane, rounded up a crew of retired pilots, engineers and

tradesmen, and with a one-on-one mentorship programme worked with nine senior high-school students every Wednesday afternoon from 12.30 to 5.00pm. That was over 2012 and 2013. The students, both male and female, worked exceptionally well and learned many new skills.

The students were treated to a trip to Auckland, where they went through Air New Zealand's engineering shops, went to Ardmore to see the warbirds, and were also treated to a visit to a company restoring a World War II Mosquito and Spitfire. They even got to fly a simulator. A pilot who had built a Van's RV-12 heard of the build and flew to Whitianga, and gave each student on the build an hour's flying time and instruction.

The Van's RV-12 was finished by the students and mentors, passed

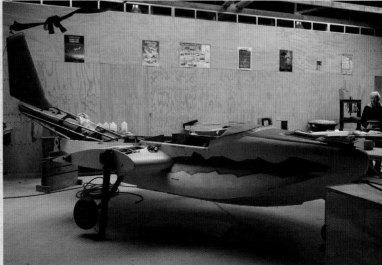

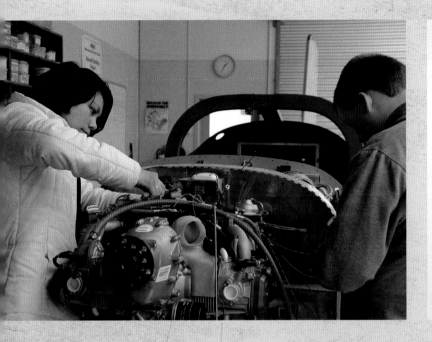

certification, and was registered with the identification *ZK-MBA*. That first plane was an absolute credit to the students and mentors.

An owner of an old Taylor Coot flying boat that was badly in need of restoration donated the plane as a project to what is now officially the Mercury Bay Student Aviation Trust. The donation came with the condition that they could sell the plane when she was restored, and put the proceeds into the trust to fund further projects. In the meantime, a pilot approached the trust and asked them to build a second Van's RV-12 for him. When I visited in August 2015, the kitset was well underway. The goal was to have the plane totally finished after the six-week school summer break. The aircraft was indeed finished on the due date, and flew for the first time on 14 March 2016. The test-flight was highly successful. The photographs show her test-flight at Whitianga Aerodrome.

Being a tradesman coachbuilder, I am able to understand and appreciate the time and the workmanship needed to build a kitset plane. All of the framing and skin are aluminium. The workmanship on the Van's RV-12 is outstanding, and the mentors and the six students on this build are to be commended. More so when you realise that the students start off with virtually no skills in this field whatsoever.

The old Taylor Coot flying boat is also receiving some work, being stripped right back to basics for a total rebuild. The interesting thing about this is that the plane has a wooden frame and the fuselage is plywood. Another great learning curve for the students!

The senior students at Mercury Bay Area School are able to register an interest in taking part in the aircraft building. The number is then whittled down, and the final students are then invited to become part of the build, so it is a real honour to be part of the team. From the first build, three students have gone on to work in the aircraft industry, and another has joined the New Zealand air force. Of the 2015 intake, three of the students are learning to fly and have all flown solo.

And the ultimate goal of revitalising the aero club? Its membership has grown, with many younger people joining, and the flying hours of student pilots have increased dramatically, with students preferring the locally made RV-12 over the club Cessna. What a great story.

ABBREVIATIONS

AOP	air observer post		min	minute
DFC	Distinguished Flying Cross		mph	miles per hour
DSO	Distinguished Service Order		NAC	National Airways Corporation
FAC	forward air control		OBE	Order of the British Empire
ft	feet		PR	photo reconnaissance
GR	general reconnaissance		RAAF	Royal Australian Air Force
hp	horsepower		RAF	Royal Air Force
in	inch		RCAF	Royal Canadian Air Force
kg	kilogram		RFC	Royal Flying Service (World War I)
km	kilometre		RNAS	Royal Navy Air Service (World War I)
kN	kilowatt newtons (measure of thrust)		RNZAF	Royal New Zealand Air Force
km/h	kilometres per hour		SAFE	Straits Air Freight Express
kW	kilowatt		STOL	short takeoff and landing
LAC	leading aircraftsman		TEAL	Tasman Empire Airways Limited
lbf	pounds force (measure of thrust)		TVAL	The Vintage Aviator Limited
lb	pound (weight)		USAF	United States Air Force
m	metre			

SOURCES

Websites

acepilots.com
airandspace.sl.ed
airforcemuseum.co.nz
airforce.mil.nz
airliner.net
airway1.org.uk
aucklandmuseum.com
aviastar.org
aviation-history.com
aviationmuseum.co.nz
bombercommandmuseum.ca
bushplanes.com
canadianflight.org
citie.monash.edu.au
classicfighters.org
classicflyersnz.com

collections.tepapa.govt.nz
croydonaircraft.com
dc3history.com
dehavillandmuseum.co.uk
douglasdc3.com
en.wikipedia.org
fiddlersgreen.net
gustave-whitehead.com
historylearningsite.co.uk
historynet.com
johnjohn.co.uk
kiwicraftimages.com
militaryfactory.com
mosquitorestoration.com
nieuports.com
nzcatalina.org
nzcivair.com

nzedge.com
nzhistory.net.nz
omaka.org
pilotfriend.com
rafmuseum.org.uk
rearwin.com
theaerodrome.com
thevintageaviator.co.nz
vintagewings.ca
wacoaircraft.com
warbirds.co.nz
warbirdrestorations.co.nz
warplane.com
ww1aviation.com
youtube.com

Books

Bill Reid. (2014) *Born to Fly*. Random House, Auckland.

Allan Udy with photography by Alex Mitchell. (2013) *On Wings of History: Volume 1 — The Vintage Aviator Collection*. Golden Micro Solutions, Blenheim.

A.E. Ferko (1995). *Richthofen*. Albatros Productions, Berkamstead.

Magazines

Classic Wings

ACKNOWLEDGEMENTS

As with my previous books, this one could not have happened without the input of other people. Unlike the other books, the list of acknowledgements here is substantially longer, and with good reason. I have relied heavily on some of our vintage aviators, vintage aviation constructors and enthusiasts for both access to, and information about, the aircraft featured in this book. My deepest thanks to them.

My thanks also, once again to Bill Honeybone, my Publishing Consultant, especially for entrusting me with this title.

As always I must thank my wife, Marilyn, for her support and for the majority of the photography in the book. She did this for me while doing the photography for, and writing, her first book, *Her Space*, that is published by David Bateman Publishing at the same time as this book. Thank you, sweetheart.

Other photographs have kindly been supplied by courtesy of Gavin Conroy, John King, Warren Denholm, Mark Griffin, Jan and Jerry Chisum, Manda Connor, Callum Mill, Chris Gee, Ralph Stark, Phil Hosking, Alex Mitchell, Graeme Frew, Alison Fellman, Matt Hayes, David Cornick and George Fletcher. Other photographs are courtesy of the Royal New Zealand Air Force and the Museum of Transport and Technology. Historical family war photographs and the logbook of my uncle came from my cousin, Neil Jessen. Historical photographs were also supplied by Jim Hickey. The original cutaway illustration of the Solent flying boat was drawn and supplied by Rob Poulton. My deepest thanks to all of these people, too.

Many thanks also to Jim Hickey for writing the foreword to this book. It is deeply appreciated.

To Ed Taylor, Graham Orphan and Jenny Gasson, many thanks for your individual write-ups on your respective airshows. Once again you all bring the excitement of these shows to life in your scripts.

Again thanks to Cheryl Smith of Macarn Design for the fantastic book design and layout, and to my editor, Kate Stone, for her excellent work and great patience.

To the following people, a big 'thank you' for all the advice, knowledge and information supplied, access to the aircraft, filling in the gaps (and there were plenty), words of encouragement, extra photographs and the courtesy and friendliness you have shown me. But most of all for your enthusiasm and your flying. I have so enjoyed meeting and talking to you all: Ivan and Janet Mudrovcich, Gene De Marco, John Lanham, Graham Orphan, Andrew Gormlie, Frank Parker, John Kelly, Warren Denholm, Brendon Deere, Squadron Leader Jim Rankin, John Luff, Brett Nicholls, Brett Emeny, Bill Reid, Graeme Frew, Wing Commander Rob Shearer, Wing Commander Andy Scott,

Squadron Leader Simon Eichelbaum, Natalia Faith, Jane Orphan, Liz Needham, Jan and Jerry Chisum, Heather Andrews, Neil McKie, Allen Udy, Andrew Hope, Jack Godfrey, Chris Sattler, Marty Cantlon, Lars Fellman, Tim Gaplin, Colin and Mavea Smith and their staff, Peter and Marea McKay, Kevin Jane, Simon Moody, Mathew O'Sullivan, Dave Clearwater and the staff at Wigram, Flight Lieutenant Dan Pezaro, Wayne Pamment, Tom Williams and Jenny Gasson, Ed Taylor, Mandy Deans, Bruce and Ian Chapman, Garry Butler, Noel Kruse, Jim Evans, George Fletcher, Angus Robson, Peter Ryan, and the staff at all of the aviation museums.

The sharing of valuable time and knowledge at the various museums deserves special mention. My thanks to the staff at MOTAT for allowing my wife and me access to their wonderful aircraft, and allowing us to photograph their museum, and — for three of our featured aircraft that played a significant role in New Zealand's World War II history and our early post-war airline operations — for supplying and allowing us to publish some of their archive photographs. At the New Zealand Warbirds Visitor Centre at Ardmore, I must thank Warbirds president Frank Parker, historian John Kelly, and the members of the Warbirds Association for their hospitality and for giving me permission to photograph and feature their museum in this book,

as well as allowing me to feature individual aircraft throughout this book. Their help has been outstanding.

I am similarly indebted to Classic Flyers CEO Andrew Gormlie and his crew, who have shown my wife and me the utmost hospitality, and allowed us access to their incredible aircraft and to feature them in this book. My thanks go to Gene De Marco and his crew at the Aviation Heritage Trust Collection, for showing us through the museum and allowing us to feature in the book the photographs we had taken. Marilyn and I were blown away with the exhibits at the Omaka Aviation Heritage Centre, and are indebted to museum manager and trust member Jane Orphan and the trust board for their hospitality and for allowing us to feature their story and some of their displays. Thanks, too, to the knowledgeable and enthusiastic team at the New Zealand Air Force Museum at Wigram, who took the time to introduce us to their fantastic facility. The staff at the Warbirds and Wheels Museum in Wanaka generously fitted us in at the same time as hosting Warbirds Over Wanaka — thanks! And a final thanks to all of the staff at the Croydon Aviation Heritage Centre: not only for the courtesy and helpfulness during the day, but also for going that extra mile by opening the doors and pulling some of the aircraft outside so that we could photograph them.

PHOTO CREDITS

All of the photographs are the work of Marilyn Jessen, with the exception of those listed below.

Gavin Conroy: pages 35, 53, 70, 73, 113, 171, 189, 315, 318

John King: pages 8, 15, 19

Mark Griffin: pages 42, 43 bottom left and top right, 57, 65, 71, 127 lower left, 166, 167, 168, 169 top left and right, 253, 255, 317

Warren Denholm: pages 195, 197 top left and right, and bottom right

Jan and Jerry Chisum archives: pages 88–91

Alison Fellman: page 101

Manda Conner: pages 145, 146 top left

Phil Hosking: page 215

Graeme Frew: page 216 lower images

Callum Mill: page 235 top

George Fletcher: page 321 right

Chris Gee: page 188

Alex Mitchell: pages 308, 311, 313 top left

Matt Hayes: page 313 right

Ralph Starck: page 64

David Cornick: page 313 lower left

Don Jessen family archives: page 177 top and bottom right

Don Jessen: page 98

Neil Jessen family archives: pages 151 top left, 210–213

Jim Hickey family archives: page 9

Rob Poulton: page 228

The Royal New Zealand Air Force archives: pages 258, 259, 261 lower left, 264, 265

The Museum of Transport and Technology archives: pages 174, 175, 177 top and middle left, 206–208, 209 left-hand images, 226, 227, 229

Wings Over Wairarapa: supplied Strikemaster photograph, page 326

Getty Images: page 205

Shutterstock: page 2

Wikipedia: page 16

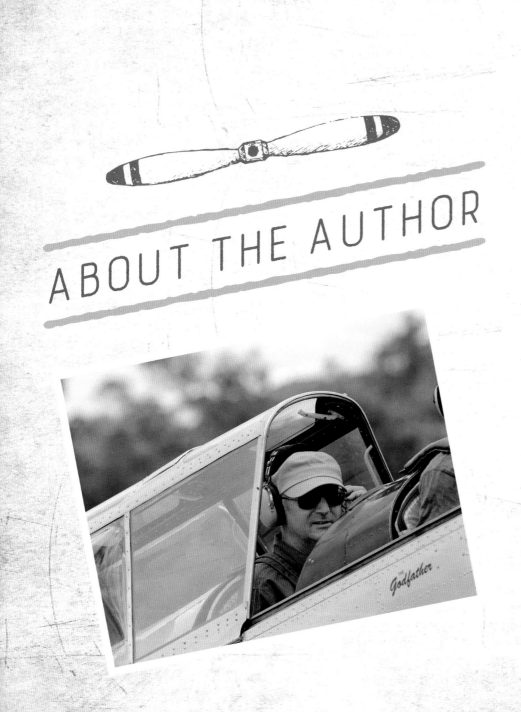

ABOUT THE AUTHOR

Don Jessen is the author of three previous bestselling books, all based on New Zealand stories and collections: *Retro Caravans — vantastic kiwi collections*; *A Great Indoors for the Great Outdoors — the story of Liteweight caravans*; and *Retro and Vintage Boats — Kiwi portraits*. This latest book, *Vintage and Iconic Aircraft – New Zealand collections*, follows on with the retro and vintage theme. With these publications, Don preserves in written and photographic form a little more of New Zealand history.

Don has had a deep and lifelong interest in caravans, boats, cars and motorcycles, along with a strong and growing interest in old aeroplanes. He also enjoys writing, photography, restoring vintage caravans (he owns three), classic cars and renovating houses.

He is a professionally qualified (non-practising) clinical hypnotherapist, and his previous career has mainly been in business. Starting out as an apprentice coachbuilder, he became a company director at 24 years of age, working in the area of production management in a large manufacturing plant building caravans, motorhomes, transportable buildings, and boats for some 23 years. From there he owned and ran companies in the areas of commercial property servicing, real estate media, and residential property investment, with a foray into working for other companies in insurance and media for a short time. Today, he is supposed to be retired, but is enjoying a new career writing books and, in doing so, following his passions.

Also by Don Jessen